Designing Cost Management Systems to Support Business Decision-Making

Pieter Buys
Editor

Designing Cost Management Systems to Support Business Decision-Making

Industry Inspired Case Studies

palgrave
macmillan

Editor
Pieter Buys
Professor in the Accounting Sciences
North-West University
Potchefstroom, South Africa

ISBN 978-981-16-1750-8 ISBN 978-981-16-1751-5 (eBook)
https://doi.org/10.1007/978-981-16-1751-5

This Palgrave Macmillan imprint is published by the registered company Springer Nature Singapore Pte Ltd.
The registered company address is: 152 Beach Road, #21-01/04 Gateway East, Singapore 189721, Singapore

Contents

1	**Introduction** Pieter Buys	1
	1 Background	2
	2 Systems Thinking in Cost Management	2
	2.1 Introduction	2
	2.2 Management Cybernetics	3
	2.3 Systems Basics	5
	3 Contextualization and Purpose	6
	4 Closing	9
	References	9
2	**Development of an Operation-Centric Costing System: The Case of a Water-Recycling Fabrication Facility** Pieter Buys and Hannelie Nel	11
	1 Background	12
	2 Research Setting	13
	3 Objective	13
	4 Rudiments of Indirect Cost Management	14
	4.1 Introduction	14
	4.2 Management Perspectives on the Cost Concept	15
	4.3 Capacity Considerations	16
	4.4 Understanding Cost Behaviour	16
	4.5 Cost Management Phases	17
	5 Research Methodology	19

6 *Diagnosis: The Case of* OEP 21
6.1 *Problem Definition: Current Costing Approach* 21
6.2 *Artefact Creation: Revisiting the Costing Approach* 26
7 *Concluding Discussion* 35
7.1 *Research Synopsis* 35
7.2 *Conclusion* 36
7.3 *Limitations and Further Research* 37
References 38

3 Designing a Budgetary Control Framework: The Case of a Multinational Mining Engineering Company 41
Arnu van Wyk and Susanna L Middelberg
1 *Background* 42
2 *Research Setting* 43
3 *Research Methodology* 44
4 *First Iteration: Conceptual Foundation* 46
5 *Second Iteration: Bridging the Industry 4.0 Gap* 48
6 *Discussion and Conclusion* 59
References 60

4 Developing a Costing System for a Digital Technology Service Firm 63
Cronjé Holtzhausen, Merwe Oberholzer, and Danie Schutte
1 *Introduction* 64
2 *Research Setting* 65
3 *Conceptual Framework* 66
4 *Methodology and Design* 68
5 *Data and Results* 69
5.1 *Document Analysis* 69
5.2 *Interview Results* 70
6 *Development of a Costing System* 73
6.1 *Design Stage* 73
6.2 *Problem Formulation/Planning* 73
6.3 *Artefact Creation* 74
6.4 *Evaluation* 75
7 *Implementation Stage* 75
7.1 *Problem Formulation/Planning* 75
7.2 *Artefact Creation* 76
7.3 *Evaluation* 80

8 Conclusion 81
References 83

5 Designing a Cost Management Framework for a Medical Scheme Service Provider in South Africa 87
Elbie Ward, Susanna L Middelberg, and Pieter Buys
1 Introduction 88
2 Literature Study 90
3 Theoretical and Conceptual Framework 91
4 Research Design 92
5 Results 95
5.1 Phase 1: Proof of Concept 95
5.2 Phase 2: Alpha-*Design* 96
5.3 Phase 3: Beta-*Design* 99
6 Discussion and Conclusion 101
References 104

6 Considerations of Activity-Based Costing in the Public Sector: The Case of SASSA 107
Mashangu Justice Maluleke and Merwe Oberholzer
1 Introduction 108
2 Background 109
2.1 Key Cost Management Concepts 109
2.2 Systems and Structures of SASSA 110
3 Literature Review 113
4 Method 115
5 Results 116
5.1 Theme 1: Dependent Factors for the Successful Implementation of Activity-Based Costing 116
5.2 Theme 2: The Importance of a Financial Information System in the Implementation of Activity-Based Costing 118
5.3 Theme 3: Efficient Resource Allocation Is Possible in an Activity-Based Management Environment 119
6 Summary and Conclusion 120
References 122

7 **Improving an Automotive Workshop's Profitability Using Lean Management Principles** 125
Pieter Buys and Hardus Oosthuizen
1 Background 126
2 Research Setting 127
3 Objectives 128
4 Building Blocks of Process Improvement 129
4.1 Introduction 129
4.2 Lean Management 129
4.3 Activity-Based Costing 130
4.4 Value Stream Mapping 131
5 Research Method 132
6 The Case of AMG 133
6.1 Problem Definition: Current Scenario 133
6.2 Problem Reduction: Revisiting the Value Stream 139
7 Concluding Discussion 141
7.1 Research Synopsis 141
7.2 Conclusion 142
7.3 Limitations 143
References 143

8 **Concluding Comments** 145
Pieter Buys
1 Background 146
2 Summative Findings 146
3 Closing 148

Index 149

List of Figures

Chapter 2

Fig. 1	Stages in the eADR process (*Adapted from:* Mullarkey and Hevner [2018])	19
Fig. 2	*OEP* organisational structure	21
Fig. 3	Operational value chain analysis	23
Fig. 4	Tender preparation value chain analysis	24
Fig. 5	Cost calculation approach	25
Fig. 6	Conceptual framework	27
Fig. 7	Conceptual view of proposed costing system	34

Chapter 3

Fig. 1	ADR process essentials (*Source* Adapted from Sein et al. [2011])	44
Fig. 2	Conceptual budgeting control framework roadmap	48
Fig. 3	Second iteration of budgeting control framework	58

Chapter 5

Fig. 1	Overview of the research problem and conceptual framework	93
Fig. 2	The four ADR stages and possible entry points (*Source* Mullarkey and Hevner 2018)	94
Fig. 3	Cost impact score interpretation	96
Fig. 4	Cost impact of the digital framework on the pilot group	100
Fig. 5	Potential cost impact of digital framework on the Scheme	102

Chapter 7

Fig. 1 Three operational process dimensions 132
Fig. 2 VSM with diagnostics as focal point 134
Fig. 3 Revised VSM with diagnostics as focal point 138

List of Tables

Chapter 2

Table 1 Illustrative trial balance excerpts 22
Table 2 Worksheet details 26
Table 3 Cost calculation summary sheet 27
Table 4 Product cost/period cost analysis 29
Table 5 Cost behaviour, controlling and planning matrix 30
Table 6 Cost driver and allocation matrix 32

Chapter 3

Table 1 Benefit categories of Industry 4.0 technologies 47
Table 2 Areas of concern of current budgeting system identified 50
Table 3 Industry 4.0 technologies meeting criteria 52

Chapter 4

Table 1 Indirect costs 74
Table 2 Total capacity per service department 76
Table 3 Hours allocated to activities and management levels 77
Table 4 Average hour rate 77
Table 5 Rate allocation to management level 78
Table 6 Average hour rate per activity 78
Table 7 Total indirect cost 79
Table 8 Allocation of indirect cost 80
Table 9 Costing—Client X 82

Chapter 5

Table 1	Channelling number and percentage changes: *Alpha*-design phase	98

Chapter 6

Table 1	Social grants by type, quantity and monetary value	112
Table 2	Annual SASSA administration expenditure	112

Chapter 7

Table 1	Average technician efficiency	136
Table 2	Effective technician cost	136
Table 3	Effective technician revenue	136
Table 4	Profitability analysis at OEM benchmark levels	137
Table 5	Profitability analysis at effective *ER* levels	137
Table 6	Revised time efficiency calculation	139
Table 7	Potential technician cost	140
Table 8	Revised revenue potential	140
Table 9	Revised profitability potential	140
Table 10	Summative situational analysis	141

CHAPTER 1

Introduction

Pieter Buys

Abstract The dynamic nature of the contemporary business environment requires a proper understanding of the importance of effective cost management. Access to relevant cost information however, is only possible if appropriate cost management systems are in place. In this context, the self-regulatory cybernetics concept, with its emphasis on the principles of control, output and feedback, fosters an understanding of the inter-dependent relationships of organisational systems. The objective encapsulated in the case studies focusses on how an integrative systems approach to cost management leads to the understanding of its role in effective corporate management. The first two case studies presented focus on the engineering sector, while the remaining case studies focus on the services sector, and then specifically a digital technology services provider, a medical insurance services provider, public sector services provider and finally an automotive services provider.

P. Buys (✉)
Management Cybernetics Research Entity, North West University, Potchefstroom, South Africa
e-mail: pieter.buys@nwu.ac.za

P. Buys (ed.), *Designing Cost Management Systems to Support Business Decision-Making*, https://doi.org/10.1007/978-981-16-1751-5_1

Keywords Cost management · Cost management systems · Cybernetics · Organisational systems

1 Background

In the highly demanding and challenging contemporary business environment, organisations are looking for cost effective ways to achieve their sustainability requirements. These *cost effective ways* however, often translate into downsizing, reducing operations and even liquidating investments in order to finance an uncertain future. Such approaches to achieve sustainability objectives are often not effective because it typically does not take cognisance of the root causes of the realities facing the organisation.

The current (global) business environment is also often characterised by dynamic innovations and technologies, which may be either resultant from internal or external stakeholder requirements in terms economic, social and environmental performances. Furthermore, organisational resilience and sustainability are often associated with quality management principles such as business improvement initiatives, technological advancement, a focus on product and service quality, or on customer and employee relationships.

In short, it may be argued that well managed, successful organisations require a good understanding of its competitive market environment, the customer/client characteristics and requirements, as well as the technological and infrastructure requirements. This only becomes possible however, if there is access to relevant information, which in turn requires that the management system(s) in place, is able to generate and provide such information.

2 Systems Thinking in Cost Management

2.1 Introduction

As inferred above, the rise in competitiveness increased the awareness of corporate resilience and sustainability, as well as that of potential cost implications associated with alternative business realities. This raises questions about the relevance of information generated in the conventional accounting context in support of decision-making. The questionable operational relevance of financial information can largely be attributed to the focus differences between *financial* and *management* accounting (Appelbaum et al. 2017; CIMA 2018; Van der Stede 2017). Hence, whereas the former typically reports on historical performances, the latter aims to provide management information in support of informed operational decision-making. As such, the focus of the management accounting function must be linked to the actual business operations in order to provide relevant decision support.

This brings us to the objective of this book. From a conceptual perspective, organisations consist of the purposeful collection of multiple functions, organised together to attain some kind of goal, typically found in some form of wealth or value creation objective. As such, even smaller organisations can be seen as complicated entities with diverse stakeholders and operational activities. In this light, two organisational perspectives are key in the context of this book. Firstly, entities are goal driven, and secondly, they consist of interdependent elements and relationships. These perspectives allow for a systems view on the business operations as well as the subsequent cost implications of these operations. As such, systems theory provides a framework within which the organisation may be viewed. We thus acknowledge the complexities of management, inclusive of multiple interrelated stakeholders and operations that are continually affected by its management decisions and actions.

2.2 Management Cybernetics

The term *cybernetics* is translated from the Greek κυβερνητική (*kybernētikē´*), meaning 'governance' or 'to steer', (Fabrycky 2014; Pangaro 2013). It therefore stands to reason that cybernetics has applicability in management. A MIT mathematics professor, Norbet Wiener published a book entitled *Cybernetics: Control and communication in the animal and machine* in 1948 (Fabrycky 2014; Pangaro 2013; Pickering 2013), highlighting two key concepts, namely:

- The importance of the control and communication of information, which links to the management accounting objective of providing relevant information in support of goal-driven decision-making and
- The interaction between biological and technological systems, which in an organisational context speaks directly to:

- The technological environment generating the management accounting information and
- The human interpretations of such information.

The above illustrates that cybernetics entails the effective interaction between multiple elements, including the technological and human elements. Building hereon, stakeholder theory is complementary to this viewpoint in that it acknowledges that organisations function as systems, i.e. having multiple elements (stakeholders) with interrelated, goal-driven relationships. Freeman (1984) was arguably the first to describe stakeholder theory. He proposed that since there are multiple stakeholders in (even small) organisations, management should not focus on shareholders exclusively, but be cognisant of its diverse stakeholder base. As such, stakeholder theory outlines the rationale of effective management as follows (Camilleri 2018; Kessler 2013; Tillema & Ter Boght 2016; Zakhem et al. 2017):

- Legitimate stakeholders, as having a stake in the consequences of the business operations, while the organisation in turn relies on such stakeholders to attain its goals;
- Value creation being derived from the justifiable consumption of resources and
- Business ethics, implying that the business operations are guided by socially accepted behavioural norms.

In ensuring effective management, it is therefore justifiable that stakeholder goals and objectives be incorporated in the management activities.

Cybernetics, as a science of complex systems (Pangaro 2013), is based on a desire to understand and design goal-driven systems. The basic concept hereof speaks of a cross-disciplinary and goal-driven methodology, with the objective to simulate cognitive abilities in attaining desired outcomes. Fabrycky (2014) has two views on the cybernetic concept, namely its embracing of the *Servo theory* principles of control, output and feedback, and its self-regulatory emphasis. The cybernetic ontology is therefore based in a realisation of the interdependent relationships of systems within other systems and that control within such a complexity of systems, is complex its own right.

2.3 Systems Basics

The aforementioned indicates that cybernetics is the science of purposeful and optimal control found in complex systems. There are however, also certain principles common to all systems that go beyond the cybernetic concepts of control and feedback (Fabrycky 2014). A basic understanding of systems sees it as a collection of a purposeful functioning of interrelated elements with the objective of altering material, energy or information (Dekkers 2015; Fabrycky 2014; Kessler 2013), which implies some form of input, processing and output. Systems can be classified in line with its behavioural characteristics. On the one hand *static* systems' status does not change within a given time period, while on the other hand *dynamic* systems' operating and flow components allow the status to change in response to certain triggers.

Research into systems typically has operational optimization or structural alternation as objective. As such, one has to be cognisant of the system *elements* as its basic building blocks, as well as the *functional relationships* between the various elements. Systems can also be seen within:

- A black box context, placing the focus on the external relationships it has with its environment and
- An aggregate strata context, placing the focus on examining the internal structures and relationships.

In coming to grips with cost management implications therefore, one has to appreciate the nature thereof. On the one hand, it is a specialised organisational function in itself, which often results in it being perceived as a *Pandora's Box*. This may often result in cost management either (i) being ignored, perhaps due to fear and apprehension of what might be released should be the box be opened or (ii) in very high levels of effort and analysis being directed to its internal structures and methods often leading to *analysis paralysis*. Depending on the specifics of the particular scenario, an aggregate strata approach to cost management may very well result in substantial operational and managerial improvements. Nevertheless, one should also be cognisant of where the required data comes from, where the converted data goes and what the potential impact thereof is.

3 Contextualization and Purpose

As alluded to above, a key aim of effective cost management is to generate relatable and dependable cost information that enables informed decision-making. Such information must be able to support a wide array of organisational objectives, from longer-term strategic objectives, through to shorter-term operational objectives. It can accomplish this by being focussed on the requisite operations, while at the same time also understanding the wider, holistic organisational environment.

In light of the above, the contextual objective of this book is to provide illustrative case studies in the broader cost management arena that illustrates how a systems way of thinking may provide a route to the better integration of cost management activities in effective organisational management. The primary objective is therefore encapsulated by the following question:

- Could an integrative systems approach to cost management pave the way to the enhanced understanding of its role in effective corporate management?

In consideration of the above objective, several independent but complementary case studies form the basis of the book. Although the application and research fields of the case studies are diverse, ranging from manufacturing/engineering to public sector services to medical schemes, there is a common thread found in the desire to better understand and manage the organisational costs.

- ***Case study 1:*** *Development of an operational costing framework: The case of a water recycling fabrication facility.*

This case study considers the sustainability quest of an organisation in the wastewater-recycling industry. The objective is to investigate whether a costing framework that is linked to the business operations could potentially provide better management support. The analysis was conducted in a design sciences research paradigm, with the objective of analysing the current operational environment and developing potential improvements to its cost management. In achieving this, the researcher/practitioner team focussed on the understanding of the status quo as precursor to the analysis of the cost environment, upon which certain recommendations were made.

- ***Case study 2:*** *Designing a budgetary control framework: The case of a multinational mining engineering company.*

Budgeting is an activity that, if not properly governed and controlled, could significantly increase project costs and result in sub-optimal decision-making. This case study's focus is on Industry 4.0 technologies, which can aid in solving this control and internal governance problem. The aim is design a budgetary control framework for a multinational company using Industry 4.0 technologies that can aid in controlling and enforcing of budgeting systems across countries. An (partial) action design research approach was followed in which the most appropriate Industry 4.0 technologies were identified through literature. Semi-structured interviews were conducted with key managers in order to understand the corporate environment, identify areas of concern within the current budgeting system, and the needs and requirements for an improved system. This data was used to assist in the concept design of the budgeting control framework.

- ***Case study 3:*** *Developing a costing system for a digital technology service firm.*

Companies are adopting digital technology at a rapid speed. Founded in 2015, this case study organisation is a fast growing South African-based global digital technology service firm that offers software development services. Emanated from the view expressed by the CEO, the current costing mainly focuses on firm growth, which was a priority in the past, without giving consideration to the appropriateness thereof. Within the context of the systems theory, this study evaluated the current costing system with the aim to design an enhanced system that may improve cost management effectiveness and provide data for better informed decision-making. Flowcharts, hierarchal charts and related documents formed the basis of the research, together with semi-structured interviews with senior employees. Following an inductive approach, principles of action design research was followed to develop an improved costing system.

– ***Case study 4:*** *Designing a cost management framework for a medical scheme service provider in South Africa.*

Healthcare costs in South Africa are continuously on the rise. One of the innovative ways for medical scheme service providers to curb cost, is channelling its members towards cost-efficient, high quality medical service providers. This case study focusses on the development of a framework that is able to identify the most cost effective route in identifying appropriate medical service providers. A mixed methods approach (set in an action research framework) was followed, with the data collected during semi-structured interviews. In designing the framework, the possibility of using network channelling to service providers was initially conceptually tested using historical data. Following the proof of concept, an *Alpha*-design framework was tested and validated with a sample of medical practices, after which an improved *Beta*-design digital artefact was designed and implemented.

– ***Case study 5:*** *Comparative analysis of activity-based costing as alternative to conventional costing methods: The case of SASSA.*

This case study considers the rapid increase of South African social grant beneficiaries over the past decade, which directly affects the administration cost associated with social security grants. The South African Social Security Agency's (SASSA) conventional cost management and budgeting approach is not geared towards improved costing and cost management systems. This study aimed to investigate activity-based costing as an alternative to SASSA's current allocation of indirect costs related to the administrative elements that makes it possible to disburse social grants. For this study, the researcher selected knowledgeable participants, mainly from SASSA's head office in the finance department with whom semi-structured interviews were conducted.

– ***Case study 6:*** *Improving profitability using lean management principles: The case of an automotive workshop.*

In a highly competitive business environment, players in the automotive industry is finding it challenging to remain competitive and profitable.

Lean management has as objective the improvement of improving operational processes, better cost management and waste reduction. The aim of this case study is to analyse the potential impact of activity-based costing and value stream mapping, as lean management tools, in promoting possible waste identification and improved profitability in an automotive workshop environment. The operational workflow pertaining specifically to the diagnostics process, was analysed together with a sample of 35 job cards. This was done in order to identify potential areas of workflow inefficiency. The analysis of the job cards provided the quantitative data used in support of the financial calculations.

4 Closing

The aim of this short introductory chapter was merely to provide the contextual setting for the case studies discussed in this book. The reader should take note that the findings, conclusions and recommendations remain pertinent to each specific case study, and may not necessarily be applicable to other or similar organisations. Nevertheless, the golden thread of effective cost management, in support of enhanced decision support, are foundational throughout.

References

Appelbaum, D., A. Kogan, M. Vasarhelyi, and Z. Yan. 2017. Impact of business analytics and enterprise systems on managerial accounting. *International Journal of Accounting Information Systems* 25: 29–44.

Camilleri, M.A. 2018. Theoretical insight on integrated reporting: the inclusion of nonfinancial capitals in corporate disclosures. *Corporate Communication: an International Journal* 10 (2): 1–22. https://doi.org/10.1108/CCIJ-01-2018-0016.

CIMA. 2018. The changing shape of the finance function. *CIMA Global*. https://www.cimaglobal.com/Research-Insight/The-changing-shape-of-the-finance-function/. Date of access May 30, 2020.

Dekkers, R. 2015. *Applied systems theory*. Heidelberg: Springer International Publishing.

Fabrycky, B. 2014. *Systems engineering and analysis: Pearson new*. International. Essex: Pearson Education Limited.

Freeman, R.E. 1984. *Strategic Management: A Stakeholder Approach*. Boston: Pitman Publishing Inc.

Kessler, E.H., ed. 2013. *Encyclopedia of management theory*. Pace University: Sage reference.

Pangaro, P. 2013. 'Getting started' guide to Cybernetics. https://www.pangaro.com/definition-cybernetics.html. Date accessed March 31, 2020.

Pickering, A. 2013. Cybernetics. *In* Friis, J.K.B.O., Pederson, S.A. & Hendricks, V.F., *eds*. A companion to the philosophy of technology (pp. 118–122). West Sussex: Wiley-Blackwell.

Tillema, S., and H.J. Ter Bogt. 2016. Does an agency-type of audit model fit a stewardship context? Evidence from performance auditing in Dutch municipalities. *Financial Accountability and Management* 32 (2): 135–156.

Van der Stede, W.A. 2017. "Global" management accounting research: Some reflections. *Journal of International Accounting Research* 16 (2): 1–8.

Zakhem, A., E. Daniel, and M. Palmer. 2017. Normative stakeholder theory. *Business and Society Journal* 25 (8): 49–73. https://doi.org/10.1108/S2514-1759201.

CHAPTER 2

Development of an Operation-Centric Costing System: The Case of a Water-Recycling Fabrication Facility

Pieter Buys and Hannelie Nel

Abstract The availability of sufficient water resources is arguably a dominant risk factor in contemporary society. This case study considers the quest of an organisation in the wastewater-recycling industry, to ensure its business strategies are attained, specifically in terms of effective cost management. The objective is to investigate whether a costing system, linked to the business operations, could support these objectives. It was found that the organisation operates as a group of three distinct entities with complementary functions, and that very limited analysis and management effort is directed towards the indirect costs. This resulted

P. Buys (✉)
Management Cybernetics Research Entity, North West University, Potchefstroom, South Africa
e-mail: pieter.buys@nwu.ac.za

H. Nel
Faculty of Engineering and Built Environment, University of Johannesburg, Johannesburg, South Africa

P. Buys (ed.), *Designing Cost Management Systems to Support Business Decision-Making*, https://doi.org/10.1007/978-981-16-1751-5_2

in essentially guessing the potential indirect cost implications. The study proposes the current costing application be adjusted in order to enable the incorporation of the operational information in decision support.

Keywords Cost management · Engineering management · Process-re-engineering

JEL Classification L74 (construction) · M11 (production management) · M41 (accounting)

1 Background

Continuous transformation is a key distinguishing aspect of the contemporary business environment, frequently as a result of stakeholder pressures in support of not only adequate financial performance, but also in terms of broader corporate social responsibility expectations. Although clean water is indispensable in ensuring healthy ecologies, the WEF (2015) states that the scarcity of adequate water is a major risk factor staring many countries in the face. As such, the effectiveness of water resource management, including its financial management aspects, becomes a matter of urgency.

Since organisational transformation and development affect both the organisation's operations and its management accounting practices (Drury 2015), the effective management of organisational costs becomes essential. Traditional costing systems however, are often seen as being based in outdated methodologies resulting in irrelevant cost management information (Tsai et al. 2015). The application of management accounting must be to associate organisational cost information to the organisation's operational activities (Cardoş and Pete 2011). James (2013) as well as Jia et al. (2006) support this notion when stating that operations-centric costing systems should produce more relevant management information. In terms of the broad cost classifications, both Drury (2015) and Jiao et al. (2006) distinguishes between the direct costs (such as the direct material and labour costs), and the indirect costs. Since it is not possible to link the indirect costs to the product offerings, as is the case with the direct costs, the management of the indirect costs should, according to Boikanyo, Lotriet & Buys (2016) become a key strategic management objective.

2 Research Setting

The case study organisation, *OEP*, is an engineering organisation in the wastewater-recycling industry, focussing particularly on the design and fabrication of such facilities. Seeing that the organisation operates in the ***high-profile*** water management industry, the provision of relevant and supportive information in relation to cost management is also central to its continued existence. In striving for the desired sustainability, *OEP* has to provide superior, value-based offerings at economical prices. In doing so, it becomes essential for them to base their management decisions on relevant and reliable cost information.

3 Objective

The primary objective of this case study focusses on whether *OEP*'s current costing system provides relevant and reliable cost management information. The problem however, goes deeper than the question of cost information provision into the realm of 'whether the cost behaviours and structures are understood', especially as pertaining to the indirect costs and the drivers thereof. Considering the aforementioned, the primary question to be considered in this case study can be formulated as:

- Could a cost management system that is cognisant of the business operations potentially contribute to enhanced management information?

In reaching a satisfactory answer hereto, the secondary objectives are twofold, namely:

- to analyse the organisation's current cost management environment; and
- to propose a potentially more relevant cost management framework.

In achieving these objectives, the remaining sections of the chapter considers the underlining fundamentals of cost management, followed by an explanation of the research approach. An empirical case study that focuses on the analysis of the status quo (problem formulation and diagnosis), is followed by the design and validation of an enhanced cost management framework. Finally some concluding discussions and recommendations are also provided.

4 Rudiments of Indirect Cost Management

4.1 Introduction

In terms of understanding the concept of costs, financial accounting classifies a cost as the resource sacrificed to achieve a particular objective (Horngren et al. 2015), while within management accounting the cost concept revolves around the traits of different cost classifications. In the context of management accounting therefore, costs are apportioned in accordance with the guidelines of a particular costing system and approach, as briefly contextualised below.

- **Costing system:** Two basic systems can be identified based on the type of fabrication process, namely:
  - the *job costing* system that distinguishes between individual production units or jobs (Swanepoel 2014), to which all associated costs are specifically allocated; and
  - the *process costing* system that pertains to production processes where high volumes of the same product are being produced (Horngren et al. 2015), to which the costs are then *averaged* out.
- **Costing approach:** According to Drury (2015) and Horngren et al. (2015), the two basic cost management approaches are:
  - the *direct costing* approach, which allots the variable costs to the cost objects, resulting in a contribution for fixed cost recovery; and
  - the *absorption costing* approach, which allots the direct as well as the indirect costs to the cost object, resulting in the calculation of (i) the operational costs and the gross profit, and (ii) the non-operational costs and the net profit.

4.2 Management Perspectives on the Cost Concept

According to Cokins (2001) a key aspect in designing costing systems is the understanding of just *what* costs are. Costs are abstract and intangible concepts—we know it is there, but we cannot see or touch it. Costs also measure the effect of certain actions more so than highlighting root causes of its incurrence (Cokins 2001). Although the concept of cost refers to the required effort in providing the cost object, there are other concepts to be cognisant of from a management support perspective, especially in terms of control and planning.

- **Management control:** As inferred above, costs (in itself) are not managed—a costing system highlights the causes of costs, and then such causes are managed (or controlled) (Cokins 2001). This leads to the deduction that effective cost management requires the effective the management of the cost drivers. The controllability of costs are also reliant on the specific manager role, authority and perspective (Horngren et al. 2015), which, according to Fei et al. (2008), Jiao et al. (2006) and Mevellec (2009) gave rise to:
  - The directly traceable costs, or the *direct costs* and
  - The non-directly traceable costs, or the *indirect costs.*

Therefore, from a cost management viewpoint, actual control over a specific cost is important. As such, the direct costs might typically be considered as controllable because it is dependent on the actual provision of the cost object.

- **Management planning:** Building on the above is the further management aspect of planning, where it becomes significant in understanding the relevant holistic cost concepts of:
  - Relevant costs, which pertains to a particular situation (Drury 2015).
  - Differential costs, which refer to costs that fluctuate between options (Roos 2013).
  - Opportunity costs, which refer to the probable advantage forgone when one decision is made in favour of another (Roos 2013).

- Sunk costs, which represent historical costs already incurred (Drury 2015).

In terms of planning therefore, it must be remembered that the monetary value of a particular cost item, may or may not influence the outcome of a specific decision.

4.3 Capacity Considerations

The allocated indirect costs are provisional costs, effectively unknown during the production cycle. With relevant cost information being a key objective of cost management, the organisation should therefore strive to limit differences between the allocated (estimated) costs and the final (or actual) costs as far as possible. This could potentially be achieved by basing the initial allocation on attainable, representative capacity levels (Roos 2013), given the context of the specific organisation. It is therefore key to find relevant production capacity levels for the indirect cost allocation. According to Drury (2015) and Horngren et al. (2015), typical capacity considerations include:

- the theoretical capacity, which is the maximum capacity in ideal situations;
- the practical capacity, which makes provision for unexpected occurrences and failures and
- the normal capacity, which considers a capacity measure that satisfies long-term customer demand.

The latter concept of normal capacity is typically used for the planning and controlling functions, and as such also for indirect cost allocation. Therefore, if the management objective is to get *accuracy* in terms of indirect cost management information, the capacity estimate for the allocation basis, should be as close to the expected reality as possible.

4.4 Understanding Cost Behaviour

The concept of *cost behaviour* revolves around the reaction of the costs when the operational levels change (Jiao et al. 2006; Mowen et al. 2014). In terms of possible behaviour, while it is true that some costs may change in response to operational fluctuations, other costs may be free of operational influences, which result in the notions of:

- fixed costs (FC), which are independent of the operational levels;
- variable costs (VC), which vary in direct relation to the operational levels and
- total costs (TC), which are determined by combining the FC and the VC for a specific output level.

Therefore, in order to distinguish between variable and fixed costs, there must be a keen awareness of the behaviour thereof. Furthermore, to be able to understand such behaviour, the measure of the output associated with the specific operations must be understood. In light hereof, Mowen et al. (2014) is of the opinion that the cost driver be considered as the 'causal factor that measures the output of the activity that causes costs to change'. Because of this, it is concluded that managing the cost drivers should be the basis on which costs are to be managed. We therefore argue that similarly to the considerations around the capacity levels, the prevailing approach must be to manage the indirect cost on a closely related cost driver basis—which is essentially the objective of the *activity-based costing* philosophy.

4.5 Cost Management Phases

Contemporary cost management literature such as Drury (2015), Fei et al. (2008), Horngren et al. (2015), Rundora et al. (2013), Swanepoel (2014) and are in agreement that activity-based costing is considered a two-stage approach to cost management in that it starts with the collection of costs in cost pools before assigning these costs to the applicable product or service. We argue that the potential benefit to be derived from any cost management system precedes these stages in that it also necessitates the effective analysis and evaluation of the applicable business operations—an in-depth diagnosis with a view of understanding the environment. Cokins (2001) agrees when stating a cost structure is created by the diversity and variation of its outputs. As such, we consider the development of an effective cost management framework (i.e. the framework that incorporates the costing system) as entailing both analytical and application phases, as indicated below.

- The analytical phase, which analyses the operations in which the costs are incurred. Key hereto are:
  - The *value chain analysis*, which considers the main functions that ultimately contribute to the product value (Horngren et al. 2015; Seal et al. 2012). This enables the identification of the i) *macro-level* activities, i.e. those adding value to the overall business and ii) the *micro-level* activities, i.e. the detailed-level activities within the macro-activities.
  - The *identification of the cost pools*, which occurs once all the operational value chain activities have been identified, along with critical activity attributes. In these groupings, they are typically classified in a cost hierarchy (Mowen et al. 2014), which would indicate an appropriate operational level such as unit, batch, product, customer or facility-level operations.

It is therefore argued that the effectiveness of any cost management framework, should be founded in the understanding that it is but a part of a larger integrated system in which the cost management function interacts with other elements. A proper cost management framework therefore goes further than the cost accounting function, and moves into the area of business (re-) engineering and systems analysis.

- The application phase, which is the embodiment of the costing system, i.e. in the actual cost allocation processes. This also occurs in two stages as follows:
  - Cost pool cost allocation, in which the indirect resource costs are assigned to the applicable cost pools using the appropriate resource cost driver (Fei et al. 2008; Noreen et al. 2008).
  - Cost object cost allocation, in which the above-indicated costs are allocated to the cost objects. This is firstly achieved using a cost driver rate for each operational activity, having a causative association to the cost (Fei et al. 2008; Noreen et al. 2008), and secondly, assigning the costs to the cost objects based on the capacity level identified earlier (Mowen et al. 2014; Noreen et al. 2008).

The above is intended to provide specific and relevant cost information for each product offering, based on actual operational knowledge. A further objective is to provide a more representative estimation of the *actual* product and service offering costs.

5 Research Methodology

The empirical research approach is founded in the design science research paradigm, and then especially aspects of the elaborated action design research method, as highlighted below. *Design science research* (DSR) has, according to Iivari and Venable (2009), been tacitly practiced by engineers for centuries, and as a methodology it seeks to develop prescriptive design knowledge through building (innovative) artefacts intended to solve a *class* of problems (Hevner et al. 2004; Sein et al. 2011). We argue that the absence of an effective cost management system is not unique and isolated, but can rather be classified as a problem class, symptomatic of a common practice of basing management accounting information on the external reporting system, rather than on the understanding of the relevant business operations. Within the DSR paradigm, the *action design research* (ADR) approach is a method used to generate prescriptive design knowledge through building and evaluating artefacts in an organisational setting (Sein et al. 2011). In instances where there the specific (research or business) problem is indistinct, it becomes important to start the investigation/research by developing awareness of the problem domain. Mullarkey and Hevner (2018) recognised this by suggesting four basic stages in their *elaborated* ADR (eADR) process (refer Fig. 1), as follows:

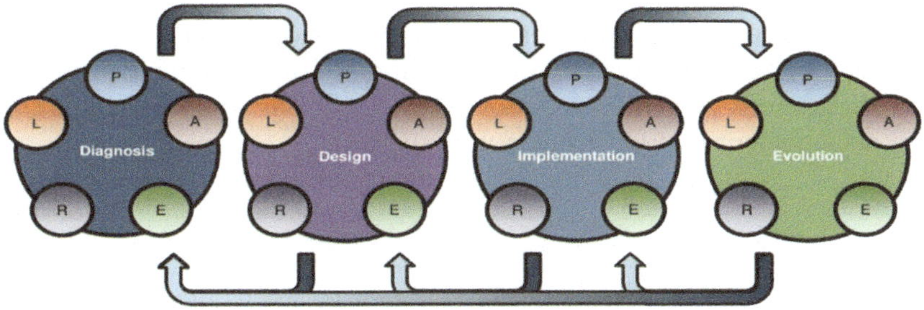

Fig. 1 Stages in the eADR process (*Adapted from:* Mullarkey and Hevner [2018])

- Diagnosis stage, encompassing cycles aiming to come to a proper understanding of the domain area.
- Design stage, encompassing cycles that may require multiple iterations of design principles.
- Implementation stage, encompassing cycles to fine-tune the build and evaluation of the final artefact.
- Evolution stage, which focusses on the continuous fine-tuning of the artefact in actuality.

Essentially, Mullarkey and Hevner (2018) considers eADR as an iterative intervention cycle guided by the work of the researcher-practitioner team, that includes (i) problem formulation/planning (P), (ii) artefact creation (A), (iii) evaluation (E) (iv) reflection (R) and (v) learning (L), as illustrated above. Due to the unknown state of *OEP*'s cost management effectiveness, the case study was conducted focussed on the diagnosis phase. As such it attempts to elucidate the problem of ineffectual cost management and developing a framework that may enable an enhanced cost management system. The latter falls outside the scope of this specific case study. The objectives therefore are to (i) properly formulate the problem at hand—to be achieved by a proper analysis of the current status quo, identify key shortcomings in the current environment, and ultimately (ii) to develop a so-called (development) artefact in the form of a holistic cost management framework, which could then form the foundation of a potential costing system.

In the context of this project, the researcher-practitioner team included various relevant *OEP* staff-members that were (i) knowledgeable about the organisation and its practices, and (ii) were in positions that have decision-making authority. In support of the cybernetic approach, all business analysis and design considerations were subjected to the scrutiny and feedback of various key stakeholders. Thus, the improvement proposals and suggestions per the case study were custom-fit to the organisation and management buy-in hereto not an issue.

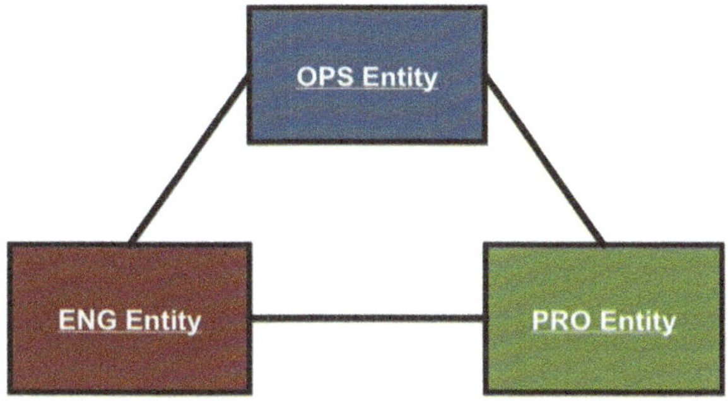

Fig. 2 *OEP* organisational structure

6 Diagnosis: The Case of *OEP*

6.1 Problem Definition: Current Costing Approach

Organisational Structure

The case study organisation's business model consists out of a cluster of separate but related entities with clearly defined business relationships, as illustrated below (Fig. 2).

In terms of (relative) trial balances, Table 1 provides an illustrative understanding of the relative size of the various income/expense items within the group.[1]

- As the primary operations entity, ***OPS*** represents the group's main income stream while also incurring the primary direct and indirect costs. The prevalent asset classification is found in the machinery and the current asset categories, while the current liabilities reflect the group's creditor obligations.
- As the intellectual entity within the group, ***ENG***'s income stream consists of intergroup consulting fees and intellectual property-related services (indirect costs). Its fixed assets are essentially vehicles, while its current assets are predominantly intergroup debtors.
- The ***PRO*** entity owns the production facilities with the assets primarily consisting of related fixed assets, and with income being the intergroup rent charged.

[1] Note: Rounding errors may be present in the relative percentage calculations.

Table 1 Illustrative trial balance excerpts

		OPS Entity	ENG Entity	PRO Entity
Balance sheet				
TOTAL ASSETS		**100,00%**	**100,00%**	**100,00%**
Fixed assets		6,39%	15,81%	96,78%
	Computer equipment	0,35%		
	Land and buildings			96,78%
	Machinery	3,89%	0,42%	
	Motor vehicles	0,48%	15,39%	
	Office equipment	1,68%		
Bank		4,85%	5,56%	3,22%
Current assets		70,55%	78,63%	
TOTAL EQUITY		**100,00%**	**100,00%**	**100,00%**
Owners equity		12,42%	0,44%	80,17%
	Capital	2,32%		41,41%
	Accumulated profit	10,10%	0,44%	38,77%
Long term liability		0,62%	0,45%	6,85%
Current liability		86,96%	9,22%	4,85%
Income statement				
Net income		**24,79%**	**100,27%**	**103,59%**
	Trading income	100,00%	100,00%	100,00%
	Less: Trading expense	75,64%		
	Trading income	24,36%	100,00%	100,00%
	Other income (Interest and discount)	0,42%	0,27%	3,59%
Expense		**27,93%**	**61,30%**	**18,86%**
	Accounting fees	0,29%	0,12%	0,94%
	Legal expenses	0,18%		
	Professional fees	0,41%	0,02%	
	Bank charges	0,04%	0,06%	0,11%
	Consulting	18,35%		
	Depreciation	0,09%	1,21%	4,62%
	Director remuneration	0,09%	9,39%	
	Salaries and wages	3,06%	45,93%	
	Wages	2,23%		
	Electricity and water	0,20%		10,07%
	Entertainment (Marketing and sales promotions)	0,04%		
	Insurance	0,27%	0,53%	2,66%
	Interest	0,04%	0,01%	
	Licenses	0,00%	0,12%	
	Low value assets	0,05%		
	Marketing	0,05%		
	Medical	0,03%		
	N/T Subsistence allowance	0,11%	0,03%	
	Petrol	0,02%	2,27%	
	Printing and stationary	0,07%		
	Protecting clothing	0,02%		
	Refreshments	0,02%		
	Rent (Wiugra)	1,21%		
	Repairs (Building)	0,10%		0,42%
	Repairs (Machinery)	0,03%		
	Repairs (Vehicles)	0,04%	0,91%	
	Repairs (General)	0,03%	0,12%	
	Socio-economic development	0,00%		
	Security	0,02%		
	Skills development (SARS)	0,01%	0,36%	
	Subscriptions	0,14%	0,01%	0,03%
	Telephone	0,09%	0,03%	
	Training	0,05%	0,03%	
	Travel expenses	0,42%	0,14%	
	Workshop	0,14%		
Profit		**-3,15%**	**38,97%**	**84,74%**

Business Analysis

In analysing the current operational environment, focus was placed on the overall operational value chain, as opposed to the three separate entities. The holistic value chain is presented below (Fig. 3).

Per Fig. 3, while the general manager has oversight responsibility, the following key value chain roles govern the actual operations.

- Procurement represents the initial point of contact with a potential new client/project while also fulfilling an important role in the preparation of the final proposal.
- Fabrication includes several sub-functions such as design, engineering, production, project management and quality assurance.
- Financial provides overall accounting and financial management support.

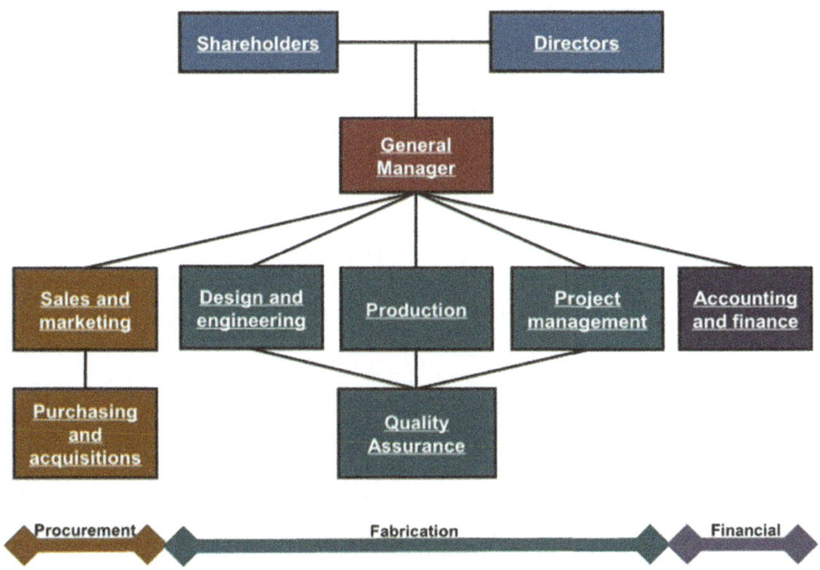

Fig. 3 Operational value chain analysis

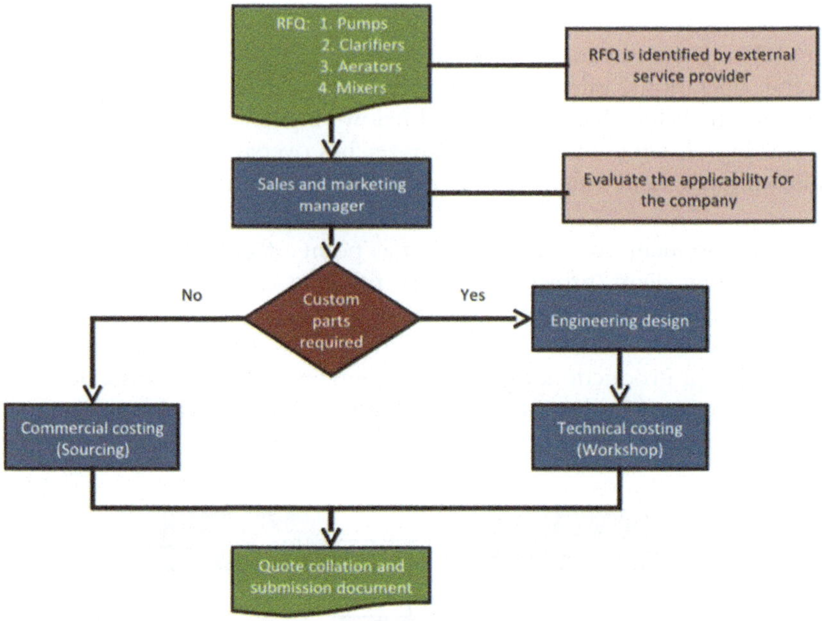

Fig. 4 Tender preparation value chain analysis

The organisation's business model is primarily based on responding to requests for tenders, in which the specific tender requirements are unpacked for quote preparation, as presented below (Fig. 4):

Cost Analysis
The tender-specific deliverables form the basis for the quote calculation, which in turn is collated via a regular Microsoft Excel spreadsheet application package. A generically designed worksheet is populated with cost estimates as per the engineering design and acquisition schedule and consists of seven distinct but integrated worksheets (refer to Fig. 5).

The details of the worksheets are presented in Table 2.

The organisation's current costing system does not focus on the analysis of its indirect costs, but rather uses a *one-size-fits-all* approach in allocating such costs without any deliberation in terms of accuracy or

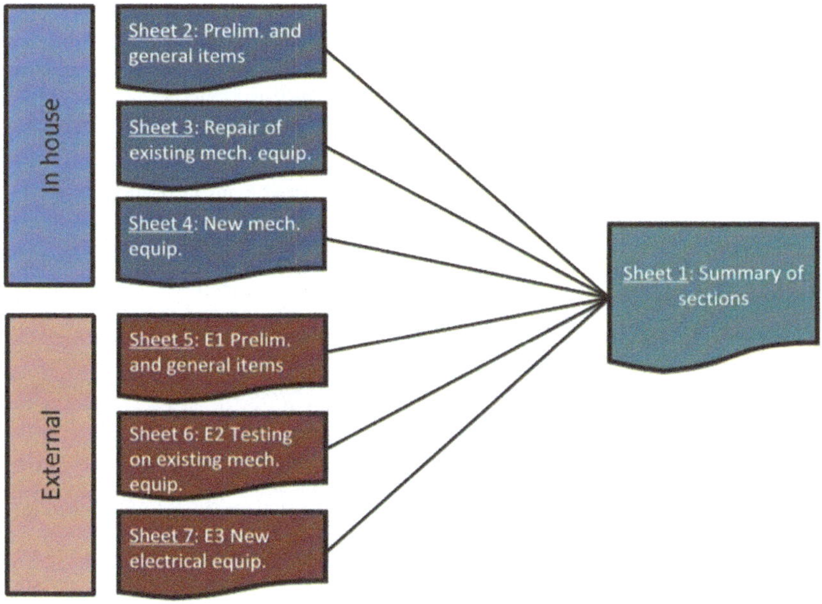

Fig. 5 Cost calculation approach

relevance. Consider the example below, detailing Worksheet 1 information (Table 2). The blue oval indicates the allowances for indirect costs in the total cost calculations (Table 3).

Per the above, the following indirect cost allowances are acknowledged:

- The value-added tax allowance.
- The construction factor allowance, representing a profit provision on externally sourced items.
- The overhead allowance, representing the primary provision for the indirect (product delivery) costs.
- The years contract period allowance, reflects potential additional performance assurances to the client.
- The design and development allowance offers a (possible) extra time requirement provision, should the engineering require it.

Table 2 Worksheet details

Worksheet 1 **Summary of sections**	The collation of the cost information per the detailed worksheets
Worksheet 2 **Preliminary and general items**	The worksheet schedule indicating the: Fixed charge items in relation to site preparation and management Time-related items in relation to site preparation and management Provisional amounts in relation to built-in costs and requirements per the tender requirements
Worksheet 3 **Repair of existing mechanical equipment**	The worksheet schedule indicating the potential repair and maintenance-related costs in relation to existing facilities
Worksheet 4 **New mechanical equipment**	The worksheet schedule indicating the costs related to the design and fabrication of new facilities
Worksheet 5 **E1: Preliminary and general items**	An externally prepared electrical requirement worksheet schedule prepared by external contractors, supplementing worksheet 2
Worksheet 6 **E2: Testing on existing electrical equipment**	An externally prepared electrical requirement worksheet schedule prepared by external contractors, supplementing worksheet 3
Worksheet 7 **E3: New electrical equipment**	An externally prepared electrical requirement worksheet schedule prepared by external contractors, supplementing worksheet 4

Once all the cost information has been acquired, a final quote, in the required format, is prepared and submitted.

6.2 *Artefact Creation: Revisiting the Costing Approach*

Cost Management Framework

Based on the above, it can be deduced there is no proactive indirect cost management being done at the case study organisation. Following the earlier theoretical underpinnings as guide, we propose a conceptual framework following the guidelines presented below (Fig. 6).

The approach guidelines offered above, presents a chronological roadmap, as follows:

Table 3 Cost calculation summary sheet

14,00 % VALUE ADDED TAX
12,50 % CONSTRUCTION FACTOR
1,50 % OVERHEAD ALLOWANCE
1,00 YEARS CONTRACT PERIOD (EXCL MAINTENANCE PERIOD)
2,00 % DESIGN & DEVELOPMENT

TOTAL COST CONVERSION FACTOR : 1

ITEM	DESCRIPTION		MAKE OR MODEL	SUPPLIER
1	1 : PRELIMINARY AND GENERAL ITEMS		-	-
2	2 : REPAIR OF EXISTING MECHANICAL EQUIPMENT		-	-
3	3 : SUP INS COM NEW MECHANICAL EQUIPMENT		-	-
E1	E1 : P&G		-	-
E2	E2 : TESTING ON EXISTING ELECTRICAL EQUIPMENT		-	-
E3	E3 : NEW ELECTRICAL EQUIPMENT		-	-
	GRAND TOTALS OF ALL SECTIONS		-	-

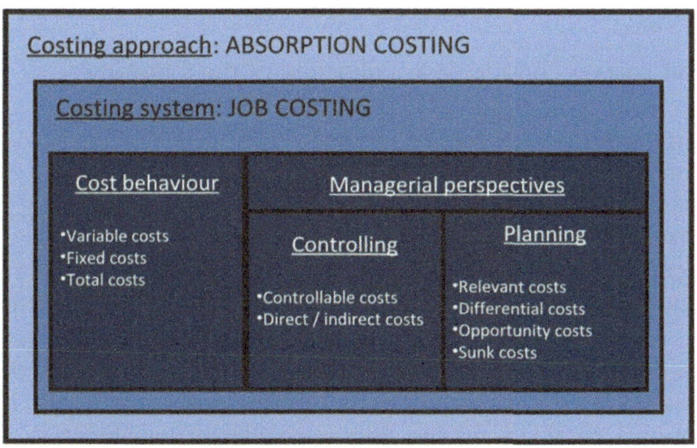

Fig. 6 Conceptual framework

Step 1: Costing approach

It is key that all the relevant costs be considered for tender preparation purposes; hence, an absorption costing approach (also known as full costing), as opposed to a direct costing approach, is proposed.

Step 2: Costing system

Given that the business model revolves around separately identifiable projects, a job costing system, as opposed to a process costing system, would be best suited.

Step 3: Cost behaviour analysis

Before embarking on an analysis of cost behaviour in itself, the trial balance layout was reformatted in order to assist in the identification of possible cost pools as follows (refer to Table 4):

Product costs is considered as consisting of the following:

- The primary product costs, i.e. costs inclusive of the direct materials and the direct labour.
- The indirect product costs, i.e. costs inclusive of the indirect labour (i.e. engineering design), the transport costs and any sundry costs not captured in the main cost categories.

Period costs is considered as consisting of the following:

- Administrative staff-related costs;
- Professional fees;
- Facilities maintenance-related costs;
- Finance costs;
- Sales and administrative costs and
- Sundry costs not captured in the other categories mentioned above.

By re-designing the generic worksheet template, two objectives are accomplished. Firstly, it considers the holistic costs role in the broader organisational context, and secondly it enables management to identify the drivers (activities) that cause costs to be incurred.

Now that the key cost pools have been identified, we are in a better position to analyse the cost behaviour. The following section offers guidance with regard to this analysis, which should always be an ongoing, dynamic management process. Table 5 provides some insight into this analysis.

In respect of Table 5, the following should be noted:

Table 4 Product cost/period cost analysis

PRODUCT COSTS (Fabrication costs)		100,00%
Primary costs		81,41%
* **Direct material**	Trading expense (Purchases)	71,41%
* **Direct labour**	Wages	10,01%
Indirect costs		18,59%
* **Indirect labour**		17,72%
	Professional fees: Engineering consulting	17,32%
	Professional fees: Labour consulting	0,01%
	Other	0,39%
* **Transport**		0,83%
	Petrol	0,41%
	Travel expenses	0,42%
* **Sundry**		0,04%
	Cleaning materials	0,02%
	Protecting clothing	0,02%
PERIOD COSTS (Non-fabrication costs)		100,00%
* **Staff related**		54,55%
	Director remuneration	19,63%
	Medical	0,35%
	Refreshments	0,21%
	Salaries	33,71%
	Training	0,66%
* **Professional fees**		9,88%
	Accounting	3,52%
	Insurance	4,41%
	Legal	1,95%
* **Facilities**		26,73%
	Depreciation	4,05%
	Electricity and water	3,61%
	Rent (Wiugra)	13,26%
	Repairs (Vehicles)	2,19%
	Repairs (Building)	1,15%
	Repairs (General)	0,52%
	Repairs (Machinery)	0,35%
	Workshop	1,56%
* **Finance**		2,57%
	Bank charges	0,56%
	Interest	0,44%
	Subscriptions	1,58%
* **Sales and admin**		4,21%
	Entertainment (Marketing and sales promotions)	0,49%
	Marketing	0,59%
	N/T Reimbursements	0,08%
	N/T Subsistence allowance	1,23%
	Printing and stationary	0,77%
	Telephone	1,05%
* **Sundry**		2,05%
	Donations	0,09%
	Licenses	0,29%
	Low value assets	0,56%
	Security	0,21%
	Skills development (SARS)	0,79%
	Socio-economic development	0,01%

Table 5 Cost behaviour, controlling and planning matrix

	Amount	Behaviour		Controlling			Planning	
		VC	FC	Controllable	Direct	Indirect	Relevant	Differential
PRODUCT COSTS	**100,00%**							
Primary costs	**81,41%**							
* Direct material	**71,41%**	X		Yes	X		X	X
* Direct labour	**10,01%**	X		Yes	X		X	X
Indirect costs	**18,59%**							
* Indirect labour	**17,72%**	X	X	Yes		X		
* Transport	**0,83%**	X		Yes		X		
* Sundry	**0,04%**	X		No		X		
PERIOD COSTS	**100,00%**							
* Staff related	**54,55%**		X	No		X		
* Professional fees	**9,88%**	X		Yes	X	X	X	X
* Facilities	**26,73%**		X	No		X		
* Finance	**0,22%**	X	X	No		X		
* Sales and admin	**4,21%**	X		Yes		X		
* Sundry	**2,05%**	X		No		X		

- Product costs
  - Direct material
    - Behaviour: A VC-item that fluctuates in line with the cost-object volumes.
    - Controlling: Controllable direct cost in terms of project acceptance.
    - Planning: A relevant and differential cost category for planning purposes.
  - Direct labour
    - Behaviour: A VC-item that fluctuates in line with the cost-object volumes.
    - Controlling: Controllable direct cost in terms of project acceptance.
    - Planning: A relevant and differential cost category for planning purposes.
  - Indirect labour
    - Behaviour: Basically a combination of VC and FC items.
    - Controlling: Controllable indirect cost item because these are not typical mission essential.
    - Planning: Not relevant or differential for project feasibility.
  - Transport
    - Behaviour: A VC-item that varies with distances travelled.

    - Controlling: Controllable indirect cost item in terms of specific projects.
    - Planning: Both relevant and differential for project planning.
  - Sundry
    - Nominal amounts not requiring much management analysis, typically independent variable costs in terms of project acceptance, uncontrollable and indirect cost.

- Period costs
  - Staff-related costs
    - Behaviour: An FC item incurred independent of a specific project.
    - Controlling: Controllable indirect cost in terms of staff being employed, but limited controllability in terms of labour legislative impact.
    - Planning: Limited relevance or differential impact for particular project(s).
  - Professional fees
    - Behaviour: Essentially a combination of VC and FC items.
    - Controlling: Perhaps somewhat controllable direct cost in terms of project acceptance.
    - Planning: A relevant and differential cost item for planning purposes.
  - Facilities-related costs
    - Behaviour: A FC item incurred regardless of a specific project.
    - Controlling: Essentially non-controllable indirect cost.
    - Planning: Not relevant or differential for project planning.
  - Finance costs
    - Behaviour: Both VC (transactional-based costs) and FC (finance availability).
    - Controlling: Essentially non-controllable indirect cost.
    - Planning: Not relevant or differential for project planning.
  - Sales and administrative costs
    - Behaviour: A VC-item that varies with the cost-object volumes.
    - Controlling: Non-controllable indirect cost item.
    - Planning: Not relevant or differential for project planning.

Table 6 Cost driver and allocation matrix

	Amount	Components	
		Cost driver	Cost rate
PRODUCT COSTS	100,00%		
Primary costs	81,41%		
* Direct material	71,41%	Material usage	Rand per expected unit required
* Direct labour	10,01%	Labour usage	Rand per expected direct hour required
Indirect costs	18,59%		
* Indirect labour	17,72%	Labour usage	Rand per expected indirect hour required
* Transport	0,83%	Distance travelled	Rand per expected kilometer travelled
* Sundry	0,04%	Estimate allocation rate	Estimate on historical proportion to indirect costs
PERIOD COSTS	100,00%		
* Staff related	54,55%	Time	Rand per expected hour requirement
* Professional fees	9,88%	Time	Rand per expected hour requirement
* Facilities	26,73%	Area	Rand per expected hour requirement
* Finance	0,22%	Estimate allocation rate	Estimate on historical proportion to indirect costs
* Sales and admin	4,21%	Time	Rand per expected hour requirement
* Sundry	2,05%	Estimate allocation rate	Estimate on historical proportion to indirect costs

- Sundry
    - Nominal amounts not requiring much management analysis, typically independent variable costs in terms of project acceptance, uncontrollable and indirect cost.

Cost Application Considerations

Turning to the actual application phase (of the cost management process), the classification of the product and the period costs is maintained (see Table 6).

- Product costs are the components that make up the total costs such as the cost driver and the rate, in which the costs are based on the following:
    - The primary cost:

      Direct material cost = direct material usage in units x Rand[2] per unit

      Direct labour cost = direct labour hours used x Rand per direct labour hour
    - The indirect costs:

[2] Note: Rand refers to the local currency.

Indirect labour cost = indirect labour hours x rand per indirect labour hour
Transport cost = distance x rand per kilometre
Allocation rate = historic sundry costs / historic indirect costs

- Period costs are incurred independent from fabrication. Based on *OEP's* present situation, the framework should be grounded in a single indirect cost rate per category, as follows:
    - Staff-related cost categories should be analysed separately in a regular fashion. The periodic time requirements per tender opportunity could be treated individually in the following manner:
      Total indirect staff cost = cost rate x hours (expected) to be required/worked
    - Professional fee categories should be similarly analysed as follows:
      Professional fees = cost rate x hours (expected) to be required/worked
    - Facility-related costs have to be evaluated separately in order to gauge its potential demand on the facility-related resources, and be calculated as follows:
      Facility cost = cost rate x area of facility used
    - Finance-related cost drivers may be trickier to identify. However, similarly to the product costs' sundry cost category, rates could be estimated based on historical, as follows:
      Allocation rate = historic finance costs / historic indirect costs
    - Since the organisation does not actively pursue sales, the identification of relevant sales and marketing cost drivers is difficult. Nevertheless, considering the importance of this function, it is judicious to keep the volumes of past orders in mind when attempting to identify the driver(s). The allocation rate for the sales and administrative cost estimation can thus be based on:
      Allocation rate = historic sales and admin costs/historic indirect costs

- Finally, similar to the finance costs as above, we propose the allocation rate be based on:

  Allocation rate = historic sundry costs/historic indirect costs

Costing System Template Revisited

In light of all of the above, the current costing worksheet templates could be modified as illustrated below (Fig. 7).

Regarding the ***product*** (fabrication) costs, we propose that a distinction be made between the product costs and the period costs. Furthermore, the product costs should also distinguish between i) the primary costs (i.e. direct material and labour costs), rolling up into a summarised worksheet and ii) a separate indirect cost worksheet. The following is suggested:

- Direct material: The current worksheet template can still be used.

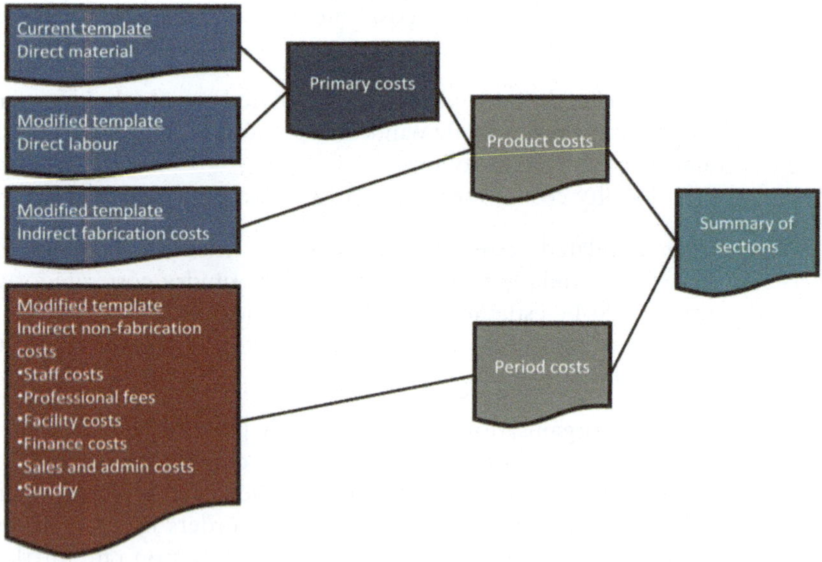

Fig. 7 Conceptual view of proposed costing system

- Direct labour: It is proposed that the current worksheet template be elaborated upon with clear identification of the tender specific direct labour requirement and cost information.
- Indirect fabrication costs: It is also proposed that the current worksheet template be elaborated upon creating distinct sections for the tender specific indirect labour requirement and calculations.

Regarding the ***periodcosts***, we propose a separate set of worksheets be developed with the intention of detailed indirect cost analysis, including the administrative staff-related costs, the professional fees, facility-related costs, finance costs, sales and marketing-related costs as well as sundry costs. Collate the period cost worksheets, together with the product costs worksheets, into a summarised worksheet that would then form the basis of the final quote cost estimate.

7 Concluding Discussion

7.1 Research Synopsis

This case study considered the *OEP* group's current cost management approach, and was conducted following the principles found in the ADR approach, and then specifically the problem definition and artefact creation aspects in the diagnosis stage. The findings indicated that although *OEP* follows a structured approach in their cost allocation and management, the indirect costs are not analysed or managed in any meaningful manner. In terms of the development of the envisaged cost management framework, the current framework was used as starting point. In order to achieve the set objective, focus was placed on the indirect cost analysis aspect.

The proposed framework (artefact) was designed on an absorption costing approach using a job costing system, thus allowing more analytical management considerations, specifically focussing on the business operations. Adapting the organisation's current approach would effectively replace the 'overhead allowance' component with a more detailed cost estimation and supportive workings. Differentiating between the cost classifications would serve two primary objectives, namely:

- Firstly, the organisation will enhance its awareness regarding its overall cost structure, including understanding the major cost categories. Consequently, the new framework should highlight important cost categories in the provision of cost management information.
- Secondly, by acknowledging the cost realities of its operations, it should become conceivable to better assess the incurrence thereof, thereby managing it better. It should also result in the more effective evaluation of individual tenders, and completed projects', profitability and other efficiency performance measures.

Although the above suggestions may initially entail some limited reconfiguration of their back office system, it may eventually require a revisit and enhancement of the organisation's management information system.

7.2 Conclusion

Prior research has indicated that a challenging aspect in ensuring a successful costing system redesign and implementation initiative is to enhance the management information and the underlying operations in a cost effective way. In terms of the validation of the case study results, *OEP*'s management team realised their current shortcomings, and accepted that effective and relevant cost management, as embodied in an appropriate cost management system, encompassed in a comprehensive cost management framework, is essential in supporting their sustainability objectives.

The results as presented in the case study were found to be somewhat unpredictable. In terms of its operational model, the company primarily responds to requests for tenders, and it does not often aggressively market its product and service offerings to new prospective clients. Furthermore, the possible advantage of being a cost leader is somewhat annulled by the uncontrollable dynamics in the specific tender allotment practises. However, the potential management benefit of a proper grasp of its particular cost structures and behaviours cannot be emphasised enough, including, but not limited to realising the possible (financial) implications of accepting a tender where the anticipated margin is unclear.

By adopting a cybernetic mindset in which the cost management system is seen as having its own goals, i.e. generating relevant cost information in support of *OEP*'s value creating objectives, a realisation is fostered that cost management is not a mere after thought. Furthermore, by analysing the costs' behaviours and operational activities, relevant information is being generated that, through a cybernetic feedback loop, will help guide *OEP*'s operations and strategies. The suggested cost management framework illustrated in this study, is intended to be institutionalised by the organisation and to be further developed within the current technical environment. It is anticipated that when more relevant cost information becomes available, the need of ***non-value added*** operations could be reconsidered. The elimination of such operations may improve both the financial and operational performances of the organisation.

7.3 Limitations and Further Research

In terms of research limitations, the reader must be cognisant that this paper illustrates a unique scenario, and therefore its outcomes are primarily pertinent to this particular case. Care should be taken in extrapolating the findings to other scenarios. This case focusses only on the creation of a cost management framework and does not extend into the detailed design and implementation aspects of a cost management system. It may therefore also be possible to identify various potential complementary research projects such as:

- the further development of the framework developed in this into a full-blown cost management system (as the final implemented artefact);
- the researching of the possible impact (financial or operational) of alternative costing approaches within *OEP*; and
- the development of benchmarking information for the specific industry.

References

Boikanyo, H.D., R. Lotriet, and P.W. Buys. 2016. Investigating the use of strategic management in the mining industry. *Problems and Perspectives in Management* 14 (3): 39–49.

Cardoş, I.R., and Ş Pete. 2011. Activity-based costing (ABC) and Activity-based management (ABM) implementation: Is this the solution for organisations to gain profitability. *Romanian Journal of Economics* 32 (1): 151–168.

Cokins, G. 2001. *Activity-based cos management: An executive's guide*. New York: John Wiley.

Drury, C. 2015. *Management and cost accounting*, 9th ed. Melbourne: Cengage Learning, Australia.

Fei, M.A., Hua, Y., Bao-feng, S. & Meng-na, W.U. 2008. Remanufacturing system cost management based on integration of target costing and activity-based costing. *2008 International Conference on Information Management, Innovation Management and Industrial Engineering*, 163–167.

Hevner, A.R., S.T. March, and J. Park. 2004. Design science in information systems research. *MIS Quarterly* 28 (1): 75–105.

Horngren, C.T., Datar, S.M. and Rajan, M.V. 2015. Cost accounting: A managerial emphasis. 15th ed. Boston, Mass.: Pearson.

Iivari, J. and Venable, J.R. 2009. Action research and design science research - Seemingly similar but decisively dissimilar. (Proceedings of the European Conference on Information Systems (ECIS) 2009. 73.).

James, P.C. 2013. An analysis of the factors influencing the adoption of activity-based costing (ABC) in the financial sector in Jamaica. *International Journal of Business and Social Research* 3 (7): 8–18.

Jiao, Y.-Y., J. Du, and J. Jiao. 2006. A practice of total cost management for integrated product and production data management. *IEEE International Conference on Management of Innovation and Technology* 2006: 468–472.

Mevellec, P. 2009. *Cost systems design*. Hampshire: Palgrave Macmillan.

Mullarkey, M., and A. Hevner. 2018. An elaborated action design research process model. *European Journal of Information Systems* 28 (1): 6–20.

Mowen, M., D. Hansen, and D. Heitger. 2014. *Cornerstones of managerial accounting*. Farmington Hills, Mich.: Cengage Learning.

Noreen, E.W., P.C. Brewer, and R.H. Garrison. 2008. *Managerial accounting for managers*. Boston, Mass.: McGraw-Hill.

Roos, S., ed. 2013. *Principles of management accounting: A South African perspective*, 2nd ed. Cape Town: Oxford University Press.

Rundora, R., T. Ziemerink, and M. Oberholzer. 2013. Activity-based costing in small manufacturing firms: South African study. *Journal of Applied Business Research* 29 (2): 485–498.

Seal, W., R.H. Garrison, and E.W. Noreen. 2012. *Management accounting*, 4th ed. New York: McGraw-Hill.

Sein, M.K., O. Henfridsson, S. Purao, M. Rossi, and R. Lindgren. 2011. Action design research. *MIS Quarterly* 35 (1): 37–56.

Swanepoel, J. 2014. *Managerial accounting*, 5th ed. Pietermaritzburg: Lexis-Nexis.

Tsai, W.H., T. Tsaur, Y. Chou, J. Liu, J. Hsu, and C. Hsieh. 2015. Integrating the activity-based costing system and life-cycle assessment into green decision-making. *International Journal of Production Research* 53 (2): 451–465.

WEF (World Economic Forum). 2015. Global risks 2015. http://reports.weforum.org/global-risks-2015/. Date of access: 19 July 2016.

CHAPTER 3

Designing a Budgetary Control Framework: The Case of a Multinational Mining Engineering Company

Arnu van Wyk and Susanna L Middelberg

Abstract There has been an increase in the financial collapse of companies due to weak control systems. Budgeting is an activity that, if properly governed and controlled, could significantly enhance project cost management and enhance decision-making. Industry 4.0 (used interchangeably with the fourth industrial revolution) technologies can aid in solving this control and internal governance problem. This case study considers the design of a budgetary control framework for a multinational company using Industry 4.0 technologies that can aid in controlling and enforcing of budgeting systems across countries. The study found that the technologies of systems integration, cyber physical systems, cloud computing, and big data and big data analytics can be effectively combined to design a budgeting control framework to strengthen internal governance.

A. van Wyk · S. L. Middelberg (✉)
Management Cybernetics Research Entity, North-West University, Potchefstroom, South Africa
e-mail: sanlie.middelberg@nwu.ac.za

P. Buys (ed.), *Designing Cost Management Systems to Support Business Decision-Making*, https://doi.org/10.1007/978-981-16-1751-5_3

Keywords Budgeting · Corporate governance · Industry 4.0 · Multinational companies · Internal control · Case study

JEL Classification L21 (Business objectives) · M41 (Accounting) · M42 (Auditing)

1 Background

Numerous cases of financial collapses of multinational companies can be attributed to a lack of proper governance practices, control systems and even corruption (Chang et al. 2014; Sabar et al. 2018). Li and Harrison (2008) elucidate that (global) corporate governance is an approach or system supporting a group of individuals with diverse opinions to work towards the same goal. There is a need for such a system reassuring all stakeholders within multinational organisations that their interests are protected (Maria 2018). AlQadasi and Abidin (2018) outlined the significant differences between external and internal corporate governance by stating that whereas the former focuses on mechanisms to manage the organisation in such a manner to meet the needs of external stakeholders, the latter emphasises the mechanisms to enable internal stakeholders to achieve strategic objectives.

Multinational organisations are often considered as the "frontrunners" in the supply of goods and services to the global marketplace (Maria 2018). In this context Beugelsdijk and Jindra (2018) is of the opinion that multinational organisations embody a social network of different cultures with different practices. This can give rise to the anomaly that acceptable business practices vary from country to country, resulting in potential internal governance conflicts (Li and Harrison 2008). L'Huillier (2014) states that the definitions of corporate governance also vary due to (i) individual conflicts in both moral and cultural roots and (ii) the expectations and needs of diverse stakeholders that do not necessarily align with each other.

Internal control can be viewed as a management process with the aim to provide "reasonable assurance" about the achievement of various organisational objectives (COSO 1992). As such, internal controls are implemented through a control framework to ensure the design of effective internal controls (Bragg 2019; Chang et al. 2014). Within this context Subbotina (2014) argues that budgeting provides a potential mechanism that can be utilised to enhance corporate governance. Hansen and Van der Stede (2004) support this by maintaining that the goal of budgets is *inter alia* to enhance the effective management of the organisational operations, services and projects. Furthermore, utilising an interactive approach, a budgeting system can be created to enhance the internal corporate governance effectiveness of an organisation (Bhimani et al. 2018; Vaznoniene and Stonciuviene 2012), hence this case study's focus on the design of an appropriate *budgetary* control framework.

In this context, Industry 4.0 concepts can be defined as the real-time integration of people, systems and information technology to improve everyday tasks, solve problems and deliver solutions (Basl 2018; Griffiths and Ooi 2018; Mohelska and Sokolova 2018; Sunil and Kumar 2018). By designing a budgeting control framework that uses relevant Industry 4.0 technologies, a robust framework may ensue.

2 Research Setting

This case study focuses on the design of a budgetary control framework for a Multinational Mining Engineering Company (*MMEC*) using Industry 4.0 technologies. This framework can aid in controlling, enhancing and enforcing the budgeting systems across the various member countries and thereby strengthening internal governance practices. *MMEC* is a South African listed company with a footprint in the rest of Africa, the Americas, Europe and Australasia. The company operates in the mining industry and provides specialist services to a wide range of mining operations, with each country being responsible for the local operations.

Although the mining sector of South Africa is facing inherent constraints and difficulties due to high operational costs and tough regulations (Singh 2017; Vaidya et al. 2018), there is room for positive development and growth if the appropriate technologies can be implemented. A problem identified within *MMEC* is the lack of an adequate internal control framework around its budgeting processes. There is a need for transparency and structure with regard to the spending allowed for projects in different countries and regions. This need arose because of varying cultures and distances between the role players, resulting in a lack of effective communication and optimal decision-making. Furthermore, the budgeted allowances and related information should be available as close as possible to real-time, to ensure management decision-making is based on updated data.

3 Research Methodology

The research was conducted using elements of the Action Design Research (ADR) approach, nested in the design sciences (Hevner et al. 2004), aimed at addressing a complex problem within practice through the application of theoretical principles (Cronholm and Göbel 2019; Kaul 2014; Peffers et al. 2007). In this context Sein et al. (2011) argue that it is important that a collaborative effort exists between the research team (i.e. the academic researcher and the industry practitioner) in each stage of ADR to produce a pragmatic solution while also contributing to the research field.

As per Fig. 1, the ADR process comprises four stages as follows:

- Stage 1: Problem formulation;
- Stage 2: Building, intervention and evaluation;
- Stage 3: Reflection and learning and
- Stage 4: Formalisation of learning.

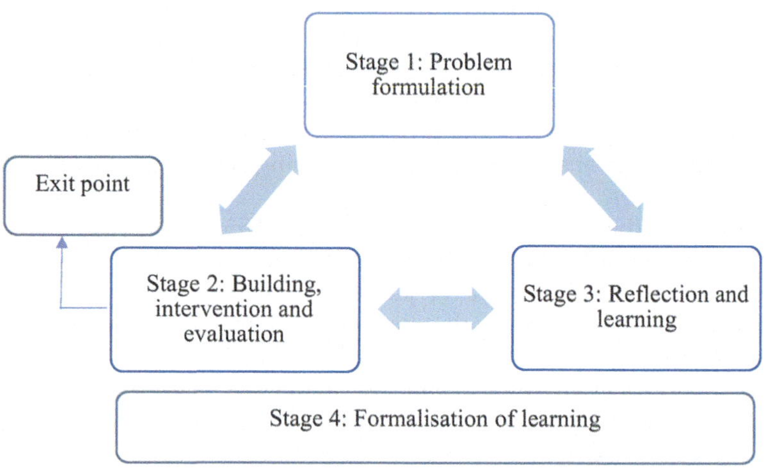

Fig. 1 ADR process essentials (*Source* Adapted from Sein et al. [2011])

Although any specific study could exit after any of these stages, Sein and Rossi (2019) argue that the *problem formulation* stage is typically the logical entry point into the ADR cycle. This case study entered at stage 1, i.e. the problem formulation stage, and exited after the building, intervention and evaluation stage. (Note: For purposes of this case study, the budgeting control framework was intended as an intervention exercise aimed at addressing the real-life problem experienced by *MMEC*, and as such the evaluation aspect is not part hereof.)

The envisaged budgeting control framework was designed during two iterative phases. The first iteration utilised data gathered through a literature review, which served to identify and investigate guidelines for effective budgeting and relevant Industry 4.0 technologies, i.e. laying the conceptual foundation. To bridge the Industry 4.0 gap, the second iteration incorporated qualitative data gathered through semi-structured interviews with staff from *MMEC*, which served to gain insight into the corporate environment, identify the challenges of the current budgeting system and the requirements of the envisaged budgeting control framework.

Purposive sampling was used to identify relevant managerial-level employees with adequate knowledge of the company and active involvement in decision-making. The following industry participants from *MMEC* were included:

- Chief Operations Manager (Africa): Responsible for all operational decisions at all the mines on the African continent.
- Financial Managers (Africa—two participants): Responsible for the financial decisions at the African (excluding South Africa) mines.
- Operations Manager (South Africa): Responsible for all operational decisions on the South African mines.
- Financial Manager (South Africa): Responsible for the financial decisions for South African mines.
- Contract Managers (South Africa—two participants): Responsible for a number of allocated South African mines including ensuring that the budget is kept in terms of costs and time.

The interviews were guided by a newly developed questionnaire using a combination of questions derived from literature and practice, contextualised for the *MMEC* scenario. The respective recordings of the interviews were transcribed, followed by the data analysis. The first level of data analysis, as suggested by Rowley (2012), is to categorise the main themes of responses towards each question. The identified themes are discussed as part of Sect. 5 below. The feedback in the form of the identified themes were incorporated in the second iteration of the budgeting control framework.

4 First Iteration: Conceptual Foundation

The first iteration aimed to identify and define the initial design specifications of the envisaged budgeting control framework. This comprised investigating the guidelines when designing a budgeting system as well as the identification and evaluation of appropriate Industry 4.0 technologies to be used.

- **Effective budgeting:** Budgeting is a key financial management tool, which according to Hansen and Van der Stede (2004) must be designed and applied in such a way that it adds value to the organisation. The following guidelines can contribute to more effective budgeting:
  - It is crucial that budgets are closely linked with strategic planning (Hansen and Van der Stede 2004), and that the various stakeholders understand said strategies (Subbotina 2014);
  - Clear communication guidelines around resource allocation should exist (Bhimani et al. 2018; Subbotina 2014);
  - Budgetary efficiency analysis should be a key part of the regular management functions (Subbotina 2014; Vaznoniene and Stonciuviene 2012) and
  - The development of the budgeting framework/system should promote innovation (Goode and Malik 2011; Subbotina 2014).
- **Industry 4.0 technologies:** Vaidya et al. (2018) identify the nine main types of Industry 4.0 technologies as (i) big data and data analysis, (ii) autonomous robots, (iii) simulation, (iv) system integration, (v) the internet of things (IoT), (vi) cyber physical systems, (vii) cloud computing, (viii) additive manufacturing and (ix) augmented reality. These technologies can be classified into the following categories of operational improvement, namely:

- Improved production, i.e. the planning and evaluation of projects, including identifying production-related bottlenecks or other issues (Uriarte et al. 2018);
- Improved communication, i.e. through connectivity creating the ability to constantly communicate and share data (Grover et al. 2018; Müller et al. 2018) and
- Improved decision-making, i.e. optimise operational and strategic decision-making through flexible business processes (Dalenogare et al. 2018).

For purposes of this case study, the nine technologies were evaluated using the three categories of operational improvement as illustrated in Table 1.

From Table 1 the following can be gathered:

- Although improved production is one of the benefits of Industry 4.0 technologies, the purpose of the budgeting control framework is on creating transparency in respect of the spending. These technologies can therefore be eliminated for purposes of this case study.
- Improved communication in terms of spending allowances is one of the requirements of the budgeting control framework. The technologies in this classification therefore qualify for purposes of this case study.
- Improved decision-making within the case study company is a key aim of the budgeting control framework and consequently the

Table 1 Benefit categories of Industry 4.0 technologies

Improved production	*Improved communication*	*Improved decision-making*
• Autonomous robots • Cyber physical systems • Additive manufacturing • Augmented reality	• System Integration • Internet of things (IoT) • Cyber physical systems • Cloud computing	• Big data and data analysis • Simulation • Cyber physical systems

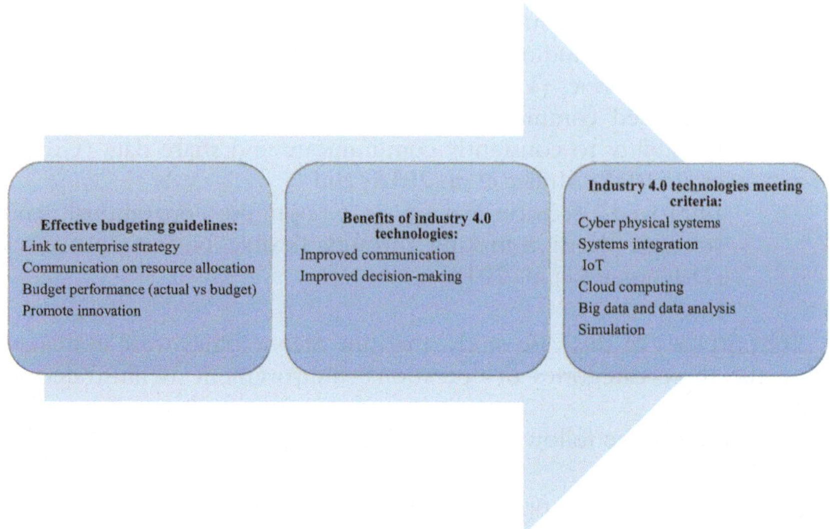

Fig. 2 Conceptual budgeting control framework roadmap

technologies in this classification are considered as possibilities for purposes of this case study.

Based on all the above considerations of effective budgeting and possible supportive Industry 4.0 technologies, Fig. 2 presents the first iteration conceptual framework approach towards developing the envisaged budgeting control framework.

As illustrated in Fig. 2, the budgeting control framework starts by identifying the guidelines of effective budgeting, followed by possible benefits of Industry 4.0 technologies, and the combination of the guidelines of effective budgeting with the benefits of Industry 4.0 technologies.

5 Second Iteration: Bridging the Industry 4.0 Gap

The results from the semi-structured interviews revealed that the respondents encountered similar difficulties with the current budgeting system and shared the similar concerns. The identified areas of concern became the focus of the design, especially as the objective of the study is to improve the internal controls and governance practices around budgeting. The areas of concern are identified and elaborated upon in Table 2.

The above identified areas of concern were used as basis to identify key characteristics that the new system should encapsulate, and were combined into six themes as follows:

- Flexibility: A flexible budget can be created by integrating systems to feed data and update the existing data.
- Timesaving requiring limited manual intervention: The time spent on feeding and updating data through manual intervention can be reduced through integrating systems.
- Transparency and real-time information: By integrating systems, data can be automatically updated enabling real-time information upon which decisions can be made. Additionally, this will lead to transparency as one system is used by all decision-makers.
- Control over spending: A single system that is constantly updated could lead to improved control over spending and enable an advanced warning that the allocated budget is nearing exhaustion.
- Standardised budgeting method: The system should be set up using a single budgeting method that can be compared across the various projects. As the system will be integrated and fed by real-time data, a common answer will be achieved.
- Interactive and goal-congruency: The system should be designed to encourage employees to interact with it, and furthermore the budgeting system should enable the employees to reach the corporate strategic goals.

The budgeting control framework was designed by combining the two applicable categories of benefits of Industry 4.0 technologies (refer Table 1) and the six identified themes that the new budgeting system should display. These were linked with the six Industry 4.0 technologies meeting the criteria as specified by the guidelines of effective budgeting and the categories of benefits of Industry 4.0 technologies as presented in Fig. 2. Building hereon, Table 3 presents the final Industry 4.0 technologies that meets the criteria as discussed, and the motivation for its inclusion.

Table 2 Areas of concern of current budgeting system identified

Area of concern	*Explanation*	*Addressed in first iteration*
There is not a common method of creating budgets	A common method to create budgets was lacking, making the meaningful comparison of data difficult	No
A single version of the truth is lacking	The current budgeting system follows a fixed or traditional budgeting method, requiring adjustments as changes occur. Adjustments are currently made haphazardly resulting in various versions of the same document	Yes, a single, integrated system will be used
A high level of manual intervention is required which can lead to errors	To ensure an efficient budgeting process, regular manual intervention was required. This was identified as a major frustration as it is time-consuming without guaranteeing accurate budgets	To some extent
It is time consuming	As also highlighted above, respondents spend much time on creating and monitoring budgets which could rather be spent on analysing budgets and improving the performance of drilling projects	To some extent—this will be combined with manual intervention, the previous concern discussed
There is limited transparency of the budgeted values	There is lack of transparency around the ability to view the total monthly and year-to-date budgeted allowance and expenses for a project	No
Data is not accurate	The regular required manual intervention and adjustments lead to inaccurate data	No, will however be addressed through addressing other concerns

Area of concern	*Explanation*	*Addressed in first iteration*
Difficult to enforce employee behaviour	The interviewees highlighted that they have little control over employees on site to act in a way that supports the strategic goals and mission of a project and the company	No
It is a static system	There is an inability to consistently maintain the manual adjustments to budgets because of operational incidents	Yes
There are delays in receiving data	The delay in receiving data results in outdated information, leading to inaccurate decision-making and resource allocation	No, but addressed through the concern around transparency
A warning system for overspent in budgets is lacking	The current system lacks a warning system for overspent budgets. This can only be achieved through time-consuming manual calculations and assumptions	Yes

Table 3 Industry 4.0 technologies meeting criteria

	Chosen Industry 4.0 technology	*Motivation*
Improved communication		
Transparency	System integration	By integration of the case study company's Enterprise Resource Planning (ERP) system and the budgeting control framework, the budget can be viewed in different formats and time periods
Control over spending and advanced warning thereof	Cyber physical systems	Users provide input and based on the input, it is calculated whether the budget is overspent or not
Interactive and goal congruent	Cloud Computing	Budget can be accessed wherever you go and includes notifications when actions are required, encouraging employees to interact with the system
Improved decision-making		
Flexible	Big data and data analysis	Designing the framework to update (based on previous data and data patterns) when changes are made to the estimated time and resource allocations, ensuring a flexible budgeting system
Timesaving requiring limited manual intervention	System integration	Integration of tender and budgeting systems resulting in the automatic generation of a budget template using the tender values requiring no manual intervention and saving time

	Chosen Industry 4.0 technology	*Motivation*
Standardised budgeting method and one correct answer	System integration	Automatic generation (no manual intervention) of single budget template through integration of tender and budgeting systems. By also integrating the ERP and budgeting system, the actual values will automatically be reflected. Resulting in a single document and limiting manual intervention

As mentioned earlier, two key benefits of Industry 4.0 technologies are improved communications and improved decision-making. By considering the six themes identified earlier, Table 3 narrows Industry 4.0 technologies down to systems integration, cyber physical systems, cloud computing and big data and data analysis. The motivation for selecting these technologies also reflect that an integration of the *MMEC*'s systems is required, including integrating the ERP and tender preparation systems with the budgeting system. The tender system for instance is currently a stand-alone system and requires the preparation of a budget upon which the tender is based. When the tender is accepted the already-prepared budget is then utilised to manage and control the expenditure. An integration of the tender system and the budgeting control framework would eliminate manual intervention and remove the duplication (or re-entering/capturing) the budgetary allowances into the new system.

The final step in preparation of the second iteration of the budgeting control framework is to consider whether the identified Industry 4.0 technologies are viable to be implemented by *MMEC* based on costs, implementation time, and user-friendliness of the technology. This warrants a discussion of each of the identified technologies, its benefits and drawbacks and evaluating it based on its viability.

- **System integration:** At the core of the system integration concept is the aim of the synergistic integration of relevant systems to achieve a goal or objective(s) (Vaidya et al. 2018), which can entail the:
  - Horizontal integration between data of different departments;
  - Vertical integration where data is gathered from different sources/processes within a single department or
  - System-life-cycle integration where data from different phases of the system are considered.

  Such a ***multiple alignment framework*** (Wolff 2014), makes it possible for different data elements within an organisation to communicate with limited human interaction. Uriarte et al. (2018) explain that the goal of system integration is to align all the data within an organisation to enhance interaction and to create improved, holistic data packages.

  A key benefit of an integrated system is that the holistic (technological) system of the company should become smoother, faster, more stable and more accurate (Uriarte et al. 2018), and this should assist in the optimisation of decision-making efforts (Wolff 2014). The downside of such integrated systems, as Uriarte et al. (2018) explain, is that it may be difficult to introduce it, since it can require multiple adjustments across multi sub-systems. Furthermore, an open communication channel between various data sources within the company may give rise to data leaks.

When considering the viability of the integration of systems, it was found that, unless the systems are unable to communicate with each other, it does not typically require any additional cost commitments. Even in the event that additional costs may be required, such costs will mostly be a once-off, and it should be off-set against the potential value created (Uriarte et al. 2018; Wolff 2014). System integration will initially take some time to ensure that the systems are set up correctly. Thereafter, the time requirement for the budgeting cycle should reduce since the system components will then automatically communicate with each other.

- **Cyber physical systems:** Cyber physical systems are a combination of technological systems and devices, and humans (Baheti and Gill 2011). Vaidya et al. (2018) consider a strong connectivity between people, machines and services as leading to higher output quality. These systems typically comprise verification tools that consider and verify the laws and standards of certain practices, such as accounting or engineering, when performing certain tasks (Baheti and Gill 2011). As such it is also conducive for autonomous and decentralised systems.

  Cyber physical systems are robust and typically accurate as it also include the testing and verification of possible solutions and then selecting the best method to perform a task. By automating certain processes, it may also be possible to save time and costs (Vaidya et al. 2018). The downside is that this can become a complex system likely requiring an expert to establish and maintain it (Baheti and Gill 2011), and the setup costs may be high. For purposes of this case study's budgeting framework however, the cyber physical system is not expected to be overly complex because:

  - The budgeting system is a single framework that will always accept its input in the same manner and
  - Two other industry 4.0 technologies, system integration (discussed above) and cloud computing (discussed below), will

be implemented at the same time and this could drastically reduce the cost.

The time to implement this type of system, is mostly required during the initial setup phase. The design and implementation process should be a collaborative effort of various stakeholders including the decision on which architecture the system will be built (Sony 2020). After the setup has been completed, time will drastically be saved due to the system only needing input from the user.

- **Cloud Computing:** Josep et al. (2010) define cloud computing as the delivery of services over the internet, including access to certain software and hardware capabilities. Vaidya et al. (2018) elaborate that cloud computing provides the technical backbone for access to data, systems and hardware available in cyberspace (or the 'cloud'). Plummer et al.(2008: 3) define cloud computing as 'a style of computing where massively scalable IT-enabled capabilities are delivered as 'as a service' to external customers using Internet technologies'.

  The key benefit of cloud computing is that it enables a *pay-as-you-use* system which makes it possible to save costs and gain access to technologies that an organisation might not be able to design or sustain internally (Josep et al. 2010). Dalenogare et al. (2018) concur when stating that cloud computing assists organisations in offering perceived value through a range of benefits which include the simplicity of the technology. The downside of cloud computing however, is the requirement of a high-speed and secure data connection (Josep et al. 2010) which may result in an increased risk of data security.

  The viability of cloud computing in terms of a cost commitment becomes clear, especially in the context of the *pay-as-you-use* model where the costs should be substantially lower than buying similar technologies and systems to be hosted in-house. Furthermore, the time taken to set up cloud computing is limited as the data will be automatically shared with all employees who have access, which may in turn also improve communication between members with access thereto.

- **Big data and data analysis:** Grover et al. (2018) explain that the term big data is used to describe the high volumes of communication and data that is generated when electronic devices communicate with each other. According to Grover et al. (2018) and Vaidya et al. (2018), big data is generally accepted as comprising of:

  - High volume data, referring to the large supply of different data items and classes;
  - High velocity data, which can be described as the high speed at which new data is accumulated and
  - High variety data, which speaks to the multitude of unique and specialised characteristics of the data.

  A key objective of big data is to provide people with enough data to make effective decisions and to gain a competitive advantage (Grover et al. 2018). According to Grover et al. (2018) many organisations are trying to focus on gathering as much as possible information to gain these benefits. Griffiths and Ooi (2018) however, are of the opinion that there is already too much data available within organisations and that data in itself does not provide any benefit. Vaidya et al. (2018) support this argument and explain that the true value of big data is gained when the data is analysed. Therefore, the potential benefit derived from having such a system is it gathers ***and*** analyses data, presents the results and then provide the company with information (or intelligence) that aids in making decisions which can improve future results (Dalenogare et al. 2018).

  The biggest challenge of big data is translating the vast amounts of data into meaningful information (Grover et al. 2018). The viability of utilising big data and big data analysis in terms of cost is that big data pertinent to budgeting is freely available within an organisation and there will therefore not be cost in obtaining. The only (real) costs that should be incurred will be the cost of data security software to protect the data against cyber-attacks. Big data may take some time to analyse since there is such a vast amount thereof. To reduce time consumption, the data may be analysed compartmentally. This could be done by analysing only the data for a specific budget or tender, which drastically reduces the amount of data and the time needed to perform the analysis. As such, big data is not a difficult technology to understand and the only challenge is in creating links between the data that is gathered. This problem can, however, be addressed by creating an application tool that extracts only the required data.

From the above it can be seen that when evaluating the Industry 4.0 technologies there may be some costs involved and initial time requirements. Nevertheless, the identified technologies are generally considered as user-friendly. All components of viability are therefore met and it can be deduced that they are viable for use by *MMEC*.

Taking into consideration the discussions above, the second iteration of the budgeting control framework was designed and is presented in Fig. 3.

From Fig. 3, it can be gathered that systems integration, cyber physical systems, cloud computing and big data and big data analysis are all Industry 4.0 technologies that will meet the criteria established in both the first and second iteration phases of the budgeting control framework, namely the:

- Guidelines for effective budgeting;

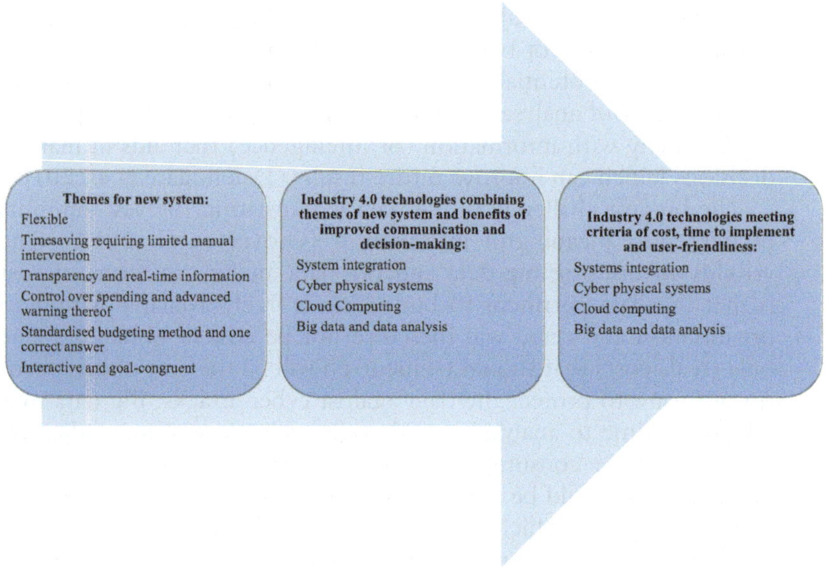

Fig. 3 Second iteration of budgeting control framework

- Benefit categories of Industry 4.0 technologies;
- The six themes identified by the semi-structured interviews to address the areas of concern of the current system and
- The viability criteria of cost, time to implement and user-friendliness.

It stand to reason that the characteristics of the identified four Industry 4.0 technologies can be successfully integrated before implementation and evaluation of the budgeting control framework in the case study company.

6 Discussion and Conclusion

This chapter focused on the design of a budgetary control framework for a multinational company using Industry 4.0 technologies. The aim of which is to improve the management and control of budgeting systems (and therefore also the budgetary allowances) across multiple countries. This was achieved by following certain principle of the ADR approach by following two iterations of the budgeting control framework.

Budgeting is considered as an essential activity within any organisation, and aim to support and enhance internal control objectives, as well as to achieve set strategic objectives. The case study organisation provides professional mining-related services around the world. This means that budgeting is therefore quite a complicated exercise due to the cultural differences between employees on the different sites, together with a lack of a uniform budgeting control framework across the various projects. A need to enhance transparency through improved internal governance and enabling real-time decision-making were identified as key aspects of the budgeting control framework.

In support hereof, four Industry 4.0 technologies were identified as meeting the objectives and requirement of *MMEC*, and that also addressed all the areas of concern raised by practice participants. These technologies are (i) systems integration, (ii) cyber physical systems, (iii) cloud computing and (iv) big data and big data analysis. A combination of these four industry 4.0 technologies comprised the budgeting control framework for the case study company.

The reader of this case study should take note of some the limitations hereof which include a small sample size of interviewees to collect qualitative data. However, for purposes of this study it was adequate especially as the focus was on a single organisation, and that the responses by the interviewees were similarly indicative of their concerns around the budgeting system within the organisation. The study was not extended to include the completion of stage 2 of the ADR process, i.e. the implementation and evaluation of the budgeting control framework. Possible areas of future research may be aimed at addressing the limitation described above of implementing and evaluating the budgeting control framework to its fullest extent. Furthermore, this study can be duplicated in another multinational corporation struggling with internal governance practices within their budgeting frameworks and systems.

References

AlQadasi, A., and S. Abidin. 2018. The effectiveness of internal corporate governance and audit quality: The role of ownership concentration—Malaysian evidence. *Corporate Governance: The International Journal of Business in Society* 18 (2): 233–253.

Baheti, R., and H. Gill. 2011. Cyber-physical systems. In The impact of control technology, ed. T. Samad and A. Annaswamy, 161–166. IEEE Control Systems Society.

Basl, J. 2018. Companies on the way to Industry 4.0 and their Readiness. *Journal of Systems Integration* 9 (3): 3–6.

Beugelsdijk, S., and B. Jindra. 2018. Product innovation and decision-making autonomy in subsidiaries of multinational companies. *Journal of World Business* 53: 529–539.

Bhimani, A., P. Sivabalan, and K. Soonawalla. 2018. A study of the linkages between rolling budget forms, uncertainty and strategy. *The British Accounting Review* 50: 306–323.

Bragg, S. 2019. Control framework. https://www.accountingtools.com/articles/2017/9/20/control-framework. Date of access: 07 April 2020.

Chang, S.-I., D.C. Yen, I.-C. Chang, and D. Jan. 2014. Internal control framework for a compliant ERP system. *Information & Management* 51 (2): 187–205. https://doi.org/10.1016/j.im.2013.11.002.

COSO (Committee of Sponsoring Organizations of the Treadway Commission). 1992. *Internal control—Integrated framework*. New York: AICPA.

Cronholm, S., and H. Göbel. 2019. Evaluation of action design research. *Scandinavian Journal of Information Systems* 31 (2): 35–82.

Dalenogare, L.S., G.B. Beniteza, N. Fabián, and G.F. Alejandro. 2018. The expected contribution of Industry 4.0 technologies for industrial performance. *International Journal of Production Economics* 204: 383–394.

Goode, M., and A. Malik. 2011. Beyond budgeting: The way forward? *Pakistan Journal of Social Sciences* 31 (2): 207–214.

Griffiths, F., and M. Ooi. 2018. The fourth industrial revolution—Industry 4.0 and IoT. *EEE Instrumentation & Measurement Magazine* 21 (6): 29–43.

Grover, V., R. Chiang, T. Liang, and D. Zhang. 2018. Creating strategic business value from big data analytics: A research framework. *Journal of Management Information Systems* 35 (2): 388–423.

Hansen, S.C., and W.A. Van der Stede. 2004. Multiple facets of budgeting: An exploratory analysis. *Management Accounting Research* 15: 415–439.

Hevner, A.R., S.T. March, J. Park, and S. Ram. 2004. Design science in information systems research. *MIS Quarterly* 28 (1): 75–105.

Josep, A.D., R. Katz, A. Konwinski, L.E.E. Gunho, D. Patterson, and A. Rabkin. 2010. A view of cloud computing. *Communications of the ACM* 53 (4): 50–58.

Kaul, M. 2014. Genres of inquiry in design-science research: Applying search conference to contemporary information systems security theory. Dissertation—MBA, Robinson College of Business, Georgia.

L'Huillier, B.M. 2014. What does "corporate governance" actually mean? *Corporate Governance* 14 (3): 300–319.

Li, J., and J.R. Harrison. 2008. Corporate governance and national culture: A multi-country study. *Corporate Governance International Journal of Business in Society* 8 (5): 607–621.

Maria, S.L. 2018. The power and the influence of the multinational company in the international business environment. *Economy Series* 4: 71–79.

Mohelska, H., and M. Sokolova. 2018. Management approaches for Industry 4.0—The organizational culture perspective. *Technological & Economic Development of Economy* 24 (6): 2225–2240.

Müller, J.M., D. Kiel, and K.I. Voigt. 2018. What drives the implementation of Industry 4.0? The role of opportunities and challenges in the context of sustainability. *Sustainability* 10 (1): 247–271.

Peffers, K., T. Tuunanen, M.A. Rothenberger, and S. Chatterjee. 2007. A design science research methodology for information systems research. *Journal of Management Information Systems* 24 (3): 45–77.

Plummer, D.C., T.J. Bittman, T. Austin, D.W. Cearley, and D.M. Smith. 2008. Cloud computing: Defining and describing an emerging phenomenon. *Gartner*, June: 1–9.

Rowley, J. 2012. Conducting research interviews. *Management Research Review* 35 (3/4): 260–271.

Sabar, F.A.A., Z.Y.S. Al-Duilami, T.G.Y. Alawali, and A.M. Rashid. 2018. The importance of adopting principles of corporate governance for the quality of internal audit. *Proceedings of the International Conference on Business Excellence* 12 (1): 1090–1101.

Sein, M.K., and M. Rossi. 2019. Elaborating ADR while drifting away from its essence: A commentary on Mullarkey and Hevner. *European Journal of Information Systems* 28 (1): 21–25.

Sein, M.K., O. Henfridsson, S. Purao, M. Rossi, and R. Lindgren. 2011. Action design research. *MIS Quarterly* 33 (1): 37–50.

Singh, N. 2017. Committed to mining research for the benefit of South Africa. *CSIR Science Scope* 12 (3): 32–35.

Sony, M. 2020. Design of cyber physical system architecture for industry 4.0 through lean six sigma: Conceptual foundations and research issues. *Production & Manufacturing Research* 8 (1): 158–181. https://doi.org/10.1080/21693277.2020.1774814

Subbotina, K.E. 2014. Modern approaches to budgeting as a method of financial control. Institute of Humanities, Social Sciences and Technologies. http://earchive.tpu.ru/bitstream/11683/21816/1/jess-8-110.pdf. Date of access: 11 September 2019.

Sunil, L., and M.S. Kumar. 2018. Evaluating challenges to Industry 4.0 initiatives for supply chain sustainability in emerging economies. *Process Safety & Environmental Protection: Transactions of the Institution of Chemical Engineers* 117 (B): 168–179.

Uriarte, A.G., A.H.C. Ng, and M.U. Moris. 2018. Supporting the lean journey with simulation and optimization in the context of Industry 4.0. *Procedia Manufacturing*, 25: 586–593.

Vaidya, S., P. Ambad, and S. Bhosle. 2018. Industry 4.0: A glimpse. *Procedia Manufacturing* 20: 233–238.

Vaznoniene, M., and N. Stonciuviene. 2012. The formation of company budgeting system: Importance, problems and solutions. *Management Theory and Studies for Rural Business and Infrastructure Development* 1 (30): 157–170.

Wolff, J.G. 2014. The SP theory of intelligence: Benefits and applications. *Information* 5: 1–27.

CHAPTER 4

Developing a Costing System for a Digital Technology Service Firm

Cronjé Holtzhausen, Merwe Oberholzer, and Danie Schutte

Abstract Founded in 2015, the case study organisation is a fast-growing digital technology service firm. According to the CEO, current costing focuses on shorter-term growth objectives, with little thought on optimum decision-making support for longer-term resilience and sustainability. Within a systems theory context, this case study investigated the current traditional costing model and applied principles of action design research to identify and develop a more robust costing system. The aim is

C. Holtzhausen · M. Oberholzer (✉)
Management Cybernetics Research Entity, North-West University, Potchefstroom, South Africa
e-mail: merwe.oberholzer@nwu.ac.za

C. Holtzhausen
e-mail: cronjeholtz@gmail.com

D. Schutte
School of Accounting Sciences, North-West University, Potchefstroom, South Africa
e-mail: danie.schutte@nwu.ac.za

P. Buys (ed.), *Designing Cost Management Systems to Support Business Decision-Making*, https://doi.org/10.1007/978-981-16-1751-5_4

to improve cost allocation and provide data for better informed decision-making in an effort to maximise value and to attain the organisation's resilience and sustainability goals. The study concluded that key aspects of time-driven activity-based costing could be implemented as an alternative to the current costing method by linking it with the ERP system.

Keywords Activity-based costing (ABC) · Traditional costing · Action design research · Systems theory · Time-driven activity-based costing

JEL Classifications M41 (Accounting) · M19 (Business administration) · O3 (Innovation; Technological change)

1 Introduction

This study investigated and developed a costing system for a relatively new, fast-growing digital technology service firm, referred to as *Firm A*. Kessler (2017) emphasises that most modern organisational theories may be regarded in a systems theory context. The applicability thereof in this study is that it presents an overview for understanding the integrated and interrelated nature of the business processes.

Since both the traditional costing system (TCS) and the activity-based costing (ABC) systems vary in their respective levels of sophistication, Drury (2012) suggests that cost versus benefit criteria be used to determine the level of sophistication when such a system is developed. During the early twentieth century, companies utilised the TCS to allocate overhead costs to its products. This approach worked well for businesses with high levels of direct labour hours set in a mass-production environment. This system changed in recent times due to increased competitiveness in the marketplace, and changes in the cost structures of companies (Popesko 2009). ABC was developed during 1987, the focus of which was on the manufacturing industry where the adoption of technology and productivity tools enabled companies to have a reduction in the relative proportion of the direct cost of materials and labour (Johnson and Kaplan 1987). CIMA (2013) describes ABC as 'an approach to the monitoring and costing of activities, which determines the resource consumption and costing of the final product'. In other words, the resource consumption is attached to activities, with the activities in turn being attached to cost drivers.

2 Research Setting

ABC is often regarded as superior to TCS. Consequently, many studies developed activity-driven costing systems for various industries, for example, in manufacturing (Van der Linde 2011), cash services (Nkuna 2018), electricity supply (Ngcobo 2019) and government departments (Bvumbi 2017; Maluleke 2019; Stouthuysen et al. 2014). This case study however, focus on a digital services firm whose operations are quite sophisticated and unique when compared to many other (traditional) industries. As such, it requires the development of a costing system with an equal level of sophistication.

According to *Firm A*'s Chief Executive Officer (CEO), the current costing approach mainly focuses on firm growth (the *start-up* priority) without considering the appropriateness thereof. The aim of this study is thus to investigate and determine whether an alternative costing solution would be desirable for *Firm A*. Should an alternative be proposed, it should provide management with relevant and up-to-date information about the costing of their services to enable them to make better-informed business decisions.

Since none of the previously mentioned studies investigated the implementation of a costing system in a digital services firm, this study cannot duplicate or adjust an existing system previously designed. A completely new system needs to be developed. The costing system will however, be based on the general guidelines offered by authors such as Johnson and Kaplan (1987) and Kaplan and Anderson (2007) and also as presented in current literature by Drury (2012). It is worth noting that the Chartered Institute of Management Accountants (CIMA) recently updated their syllabus to include finance in a digital world with a focus on the use of digital technology (CIMA 2019). Therefore, the development and implementation of a costing system and the impact of the digital world will influence the conventional role of financial management (Bhimani and Bromwich 2009). For purposes of this case study therefore, the research question is stated as follows:

> *What should a costing system for a digital technology service firm look like?*

3 Conceptual Framework

Companies are adopting digital technologies at a rapid speed, with business spending on technology transformation reaching $1.25 trillion in 2019 (IDC 2018). Digital technologies are also expected to increase at an annual compound growth rate of 16.7% for the period 2017 to 2022 (IDC 2018). The result of the worldwide spending on digital technologies indicates that it is becoming part of core business operating systems. According to a 2019 report, approximately 79% of the business and IT executives worldwide confirmed that Social, Mobile, Analytics and Cloud (SMAC) digital technology is part of their companies' fundamental technology pillar (Accenture 2019).

The movement to digital technology resulted in *Firm A* expanding into 14 different industry sectors and growing from 8 to 200+ staff internationally over the past 18 months. The firm competes in a highly competitive global market. Increasing global competitiveness has forced many organisations to render services at a competitive cost and price, which require service providers to adopt a more proactive approach to cost management (Aguilar and Ittner 2018). The allocation of overheads and direct cost should be reviewed to establish where resources are not optimally utilised.

The use of the systems theory as a conceptual framework is an under-explored theory in management studies, seemingly owing to its integrated approach, which holds much promise to improve the long-term sustainability for managers (Teece 2018). Systems thinking was applied within the systems theory approach to identify elements that are related towards a suitable costing system.

According the so-called Hutchins framework, the systems theory could be divided into the following four components (Hutchins 1996):

- The description of the aspects/nature of the specific system;
- The explanation of how the components in the system interact;
- The determination whether the system is effective and
- The identification to which extent the systems can function in practice, compared to the ideal jointed use of archival material.

The consideration of these components are very pertinent in the context of costing systems. A study by Gunasekaran et al. (2005) confirms this when high-lighting that the development of new costing systems is important to businesses, due to:

- Inaccurate product costing systems;
- Current costing systems are not improved or updated;
- Large sections of costs are presented by overheads and
- Insufficient non-financial information.

Therefore, the need for the development of new and suitable costing systems has become essential in the present-day business environment for each specific industry. As alluded to above, research by Bvumbi (2017), Malukele (2019), Nkuna (2018), Ngcobo (2019), Stouthuysen et al. (2014) and Van der Linde (2011) investigated reasons and benefits of implementing alternative versions of ABC, covering a variety of industries. There is thus clear evidence from the literature that ABC is globally a well-established and researched field favoured by various industries. In an attempt to simplify the complexity of activity cost calculations, Kaplan and Anderson (2007) developed the Time-Driven Activity-Based Costing (TDABC) system. This costing system requires managers to predict the capacity of the supplied resources as a percentage of the total capacity (Szychta 2010). Compared to *conventional* ABC that allocates cost drivers to activity cost pools, TDABC focusses on activity times (Kaplan and Anderson 2007). Time is the primary and main cost driver of TDABC, which makes the design of the costing less cumbersome (Kaplan and Anderson 2007).

A global cost management survey conducted by Deloitte (2019) revealed that many companies that apply cost management systems did not meet their cost targets. The survey indicated that the information systems used to support high-quality cost management decision-making are considered to be a key element of a successful business. The survey further revealed that companies achieving cost targets used new digital technologies. These technologies had a direct impact on the accuracy of forecasting and budgets.

Therefore, it can be concluded that each industry (and even organisations within the various industries) is unique. As an Industry 4.0 digital technology organisation, *Firm A* will also face its own unique set of challenges with its costing system.

4 Methodology and Design

Qualitative data was gathered through (i) document analysis, which include flowcharts, hierarchal charts, general ledger, cost reports and budgets and (ii) semi-structured face-to-face interviews with open-ended questions. The interviews included the following senior personnel:

- Chief Technology Officer: Responsible for technology development and understanding the technological flow of the firm;
- Chief Financial Officer: Responsible for managing the firm's finances and understanding the financial flow of the firm;
- Head of Project Management: Responsible for managing multiple projects at one time to ensure that the projects succeed;
- Head of Human Resource Management: Responsible for managing the procurement and recruitment process and for maintaining human resources and
- Head of Financial Management: Responsible for managing the financial planning and directing and controlling the financial activities.

Interviews with the above-mentioned participants were recorded and analysed. Content analysis helped to identify possible cost relationships in the collected qualitative data. The feedback obtained from the participants was further supported by a document analysis of the financial and related records. Following on from the interview questions, principles of the action design research approach (ADR) was used to build the new costing system (artefact). The ADR process model is a four-stage approach that includes the following stages:

- The ***diagnosis stage*** is the part of the process to discover and define the problem domain in which the process is going to be operating.
- The ***design stage*** is part of the problem-solving part as the research project is evolving. The design stage also includes design principles, methods, systems and the implementation methods that are going to be used.
- The ***implementation stage*** is where the artefact is engaged in building and implementing the project/model. Therefore, the artefacts in the ADR implementation stage can be systems, programmes, databases, algorithms and/or processes.

- The ***evolution stage*** of the artefact occurs over a period of time, as the problem environment changes and the artefact solution develops to meet these changes (and can be a more long-term stage).

Mullarkey and Hevner (2019) used this model to develop an elaborated action design research (eADR) process model, with each of the four stages including the following five phases:

- Problem formulation and planning;
- Artefact creation;
- Evaluation;
- Reflection and
- Learning.

Since the problem at hand was already known, this case study bypassed the diagnosis stage. The entry point was therefore the design stage followed by the implementation stage. Also, since this is a first implementation iterations, the evolution stage were not part of this specific case study.

5 Data and Results

5.1 Document Analysis

After the documents had been inspected, reviewed and used, they revealed the firm's value chain which gave an idea of its types of services, products, software, hardware, functions, departments, activities, etc. that could give an indication of how the firm's operations and flows are working. Firm A's value chain is split into two main segments, namely Strategic Management and Implementation Management.

Strategic Management: Firstly, the Human Resource Management department identifies the opportunity that has been created and, therefore, determines whether Firm A is fully adequate and equipped to perform the service as requested by a client. The type of solution that is required for the suggested problem should then be decided, namely whether it is software, hardware or a mix. The innovative/software development is mostly done by a solutions architect in order to find the recommended software to solve the problem. Thereafter, the hardware component (if needed) is developed to fit the specific solution/software that is required to operate.

Implementation Management: The second segment entails the implementation of the solution service/product to be implemented for the client. This allows the business support function to start the implementation phase and to decide whether specific activities should be outsourced to reduce the workload.

Furthermore, documents were helpful in identifying ten departments and their specific activities. The departments indicated that four are the service departments that deliver the service to clients and six are supporting departments to the service departments:

i. Finance (Supporting)
ii. Human Resource Management/HR (Supporting)
iii. Information Technology/IT (Service)
iv. Sales (Service)
v. Operations (Service)
vi. Product Engineers (Service)
vii. Projects (Supporting)
viii. Legal (Supporting department with no trace towards a specific service department)
ix. Marketing (Supporting)
x. CEO Office (Supporting department with no trace towards a specific service department).

5.2 Interview Results

The semi-structured interviews included structured and verbal responses. The structured responses were only 'yes' or 'no' answers. When the answer was yes, the participants had to reason why they said yes. The verbal responses were open-ended responses that enabled the researcher to understand the firm's activities, processes and internal operating systems.

The structured response in the semi-structured interview showed that four of the respondents indicated that high implementation cost of a new costing system was a concern and all five of the respondents indicated that the lack of time was concern. The whole firm operates in real-time feedback services, thus indicating that time is an important factor for Firm A.

Furthermore, 'the lack of top management support' and 'not capable to implement the costing system' were of no concern to any of the respondents. This showed that Firm A's top management would support the initiative and the implementation of the newly developed costing system.

The verbal response interviews were coded into themes, in the same way as done by Maluleke (2019) and Tilo (2017), but more specifically Maluleke's (2019) study, by using voice-recording to code the data into sub-themes.

A data table was developed to record the feedback of the transcripts to be analysed. The table contains the verbatim feedback and information obtained from each participant. Some themes were merged, owing to participants' comments that were regarded as out-of-context. The comments were captured in three columns, namely themes, sub-themes and verbatim responses. The five participants' feedback was cross-referenced in the table.

In order to capture the participants' experience and feedback from the interviews, the following themes and sub-themes were structured:

- Theme 1: The appropriateness, applicability and efficiency of the current allocation costing system.
  - The current software system used for costing.
  - Specific main activities and cost pools taking place when the service is delivered.
  - The flow of cost/activities/works in Firm A's system/processes/operations.
  - The accuracy and sufficiency of information available to make strategic decisions.

- Theme 2: The development/improvements from the old to the new costing system.
  - New customised costing system should be considered.
  - How sophisticated the firm's costing should be.
  - Improvements that could be made to the current allocation system.

- Theme 3: The use of costing systems in general and the management tool thereof.

- The purpose of costing and examples thereof.
- Examples of cost items in the cost hierarchy levels.
- Which team/individuals should be recommended for the costing system initiative.
- Expectation regarding the efficiency aspect of the costing system.
- Costing system as a management tool improves budgeting, decision-making and monitoring controls.

• Theme 4: Participants' open-ended discussion.

  - Anything else that the participant wanted to add or mention to the interviewee on this topic.

The verbal responses gave the authors a better understanding of the current costing system and the flow of activities in Firm A. Throughout the interviews, it was shown that Firm A is innovative and open to adapt to any situation. The main activity driver in Firm A is mostly time-driven, as the software services are maintained through teams (amount of time used by employee, for example). The main aspect that stood out was that Firm A currently does not cost its customer service, installation teams, project management teams and revisits. Therefore, it does not know how much these departments/sections affect their costing (or how much it costs the firm; it is currently just an estimated amount). There was an urge that the costing system, currently a manual system, should be converted to an automated system. Furthermore, the current costing system is not linked to or integrated with their ERP system, although they are in the process of changing this during the next six months. They struggle to adapt the costing system, because every client's needs are different. They still need to resolve this challenge since the estimated amount is included in the costing calculation for clients. It was clarified during the interviews that Firm A expected an 80% accuracy from the costing system versus actual costs. They would rather sacrifice 20% accuracy for a system that is automated, quick, responsive and flexible. Yet again, because of Firm A's rapid growth nationally and internationally, they want to benchmark/compare/evaluate their systems against international standards.

Therefore, the most applicable costing system to be implemented for Firm A is TDABC. As indicated above, the main activity driver in Firm A is mostly time-driven and TDABC would allow for more accurate cost/time allocation in the different departments. This should indicate how much time is consumed by each department, activity and management level.

6 Development of a Costing System

6.1 *Design Stage*

The design stage provides a set of activities over the search area of possible design solutions. Through one or more iterative cycles within the design stage, problem formulation, artefact creation and evaluation would be used within the cycle towards the implementation of the costing system for Firm A. Human cognitive and social skills would be added to make accurate contributions to both the problem environment and the knowledge base section (Hevner et al. 2004). In TDABC, the direct method was used, meaning that the supporting department's direct cost was to be included in the indirect cost pools. It would then be allocated to the specific service departments.

6.2 *Problem Formulation/Planning*

In the problem formulation/planning stage, the following steps were used to develop the specific TDABC system for Firm A, which were the results of the interviews and documents analysis. The steps are to determine:

i. Working hours per year
ii. The number of employees in Firm A and the allocation thereof to each department
iii. Current costing per department
iv. Average rate per management level (top, middle, first)
v. Each department's activities and time consumption
vi. Each activity's top-level, middle-level and first-level time consumption
vii. Average rate and prospective times.

6.3 *Artefact Creation*

Artefact creation in the design stage enabled the authors to illustrate how the costing system would be developed and how the planning phase would develop practically into artefact creation in order to ensure that the artefact creation is built into the implementation phase.

The flow of TDABC was developed through the supporting departments and allocated firstly to the service departments, then to the activities within each department; thereafter, it was divided between the three management levels. The identified management levels are top, middle and first-level. The cost object is the client that makes use of Firm A's services.

The employee capacity per year should be calculated before the allocation process could start. For illustration, the authors used 250 working days per year multiplied by the active working hours per day, which is 8 hours. Therefore, the capacity is 2 000 hours per employee per year. Note that it should be less than 2 000 hours since lead time was ignored and the resultant calculation was not part of the scope of this study.

Furthermore, part of this step also included the apportionment of firm-wide indirect (overhead) costs to the departments. The indirect cost (which includes property rent, water and electricity, computer depreciation and insurance) of the costing system was calculated through the direct method. Table 1 indicates the indirect costs with its appropriate capacity and estimated total cost per month.

In order to commence implementing the costing system (direct labour), the following segments should be calculated before moving onto the next segments: firstly, the departmental capacity; then the activity capacity; thereafter, management usage (per management level); and, lastly, management cost (per management level).

Table 1 Indirect costs

Indirect costs	*Capacity*	*Total costs*	*Cost per unit*
Property Rent (m^2)	4 000	R300 000	R75
Water and Electricity (kw)	15 000	R30 000	R2
Computer Depreciation (units)	300	R4 500 000	R15 000

Source Compiled by authors from accumulated data

6.4 *Evaluation*

The costing system was evaluated against a potential client as a practical example. Therefore, it should clearly illustrate how the costing system would work and which aspects should be considered when it is being used.

7 Implementation Stage

In the implementation cycles, the authors engaged in building and evaluating the given networking and/or accounting information in order to develop the costing system. Such artefacts indicate that the ADR implementation cycle includes systems, algorithms, programmes, databases and processes. Throughout one or more iterative cycles within the implementation stage, problem formulation, artefact creation and evaluation were used within a cycle towards the development of the costing system for Firm A.

7.1 *Problem Formulation/Planning*

In the first step of the implementation phase, problem formulation needed to be done prior to artefact creation. Consequently, time allocation had to be done before cost allocation could take place; hence the total capacity had to be determined in each service department (Table 2).

Each of the service departments' total hours/capacity could be determined and the allocation process could continue to allocate hours to the specific activity and management level. It is important to point out that top-level, middle-level and first-level cannot equally be divided into a specific level per employee. Although there is segregation of duties between the different levels, there will always be some overlapping of duties. For example, a top-level manager will also execute some administrative tasks that usually are regarded as first-level management responsibility. The next step was to convert the percentages into hours for all four service departments. As a result of space restriction, only the results of the IT department are shown in Table 3.

Table 2 Total capacity per service department

Department	*Number of employees*	*Hours per employee*	*Total hours*	*Activity capacity (%)*	*Top level (%)*	*Middle level (%)*	*First level (%)*
IT	4	2 000	8 000	Smart solutions (20)	60	30	10
				Network and Internet (30)	60	30	10
				Infrastructure (30)	60	30	10
				Security (20)	60	30	10
Sales	96	2 000	192 000	Service sales (33)	10	15	75
				Client management (33)	5	10	85
				Pre-sales (29)	2	20	78
				Strategy (5)	95	5	0
Operations	20	2 000	40 000	Deliverables (50)	20	40	40
				Strategic planning (10)	95	5	0
				Project drafts (30)	5	40	55
				RAC (10)	10	50	40
Engineering	82	2 000	164 000	Deliverables (70)	10	20	70
				Strategic planning (5)	95	5	0
				Project drafts (20)	5	15	80
				Evaluations (5%)	30	0	70

Source Compiled by authors from accumulated data

7.2 *Artefact Creation*

In the artefact creation phase, the costing system was implemented with the cost allocation distributed to each activity. The average hour rate for top, middle and first-level was costed as R2 515 (R5 030 869/2 000), R879 and R380. This is the average annual salary divided by 2 000 hours (Table 4).

Table 3 Hours allocated to activities and management levels

Department	*Total hours*	*Activity capacity (%)*	*Activity capacity hours*	*Top level*	*Middle level*	*First level*
IT	8 000	Smart solutions (20)	1 600*	960**	480	160
		Network and Internet (30)	2 400	1 440	720	240
		Infrastructure (30)	2 400	1 440	720	240
		Security (20)	1 600	960	480	160
			8 000			

(*20% × 8 000; **60% × 1 600)

Source Compiled by authors from accumulated data

Table 4 Average hour rate

Department	*Management level*	*Rand value*
Average annual salary in each level	Top	5 030 869
	Middle	1 758 892
	First	759 005
Average hourly rate (2 000 h)	Top	2 515
	Middle	879
	First	380

Source Compiled by authors from accumulated data

The average hour rates were allocated to top, middle and first-level. The direct labour of the service department's costing system was fully developed, as indicated in Table 5. Again, the exercise was done for all four service departments; however, only the results of the IT department are shown.

The activity cost per year could be calculated, which enabled the costing system to calculate the average hour rate per activity (Table 6).

Thus, the direct labour in the service departments was calculated to the specific activity in each department. The supporting departments' direct labour was included in the indirect cost pools, which was allocated to the four service departments (Table 7).

Table 5 Rate allocation to management level

Department	*Total hours*	*Activity capacity (%)*	*Top level*	*Middle level*	*First level*	*Activity cost per year*
IT	8 000	Smart solutions (20)	R2 414 400*	R421 920	R60 800	R2 897 120
		Network and Internet (30)	R3 621 600	R632 880	R91 200	R4 345 680
		Infrastructure (30)	R3 621 600	R632 880	R91 200	R4 345 680
		Security (20)	R2 414 400	R421 920	R60 800	R2 897 120
						R14 485 600

(*R2 515 [from Table 4] × 960 hours [from Table 3])
Source Compiled by authors from accumulated data

Table 6 Average hour rate per activity

Department	*Total hours*	*Activity capacity (%)*	*Activity capacity hours*	*Activity cost per year*	*Average rate per hour*
IT	8 000	Smart solutions (20)	1 600	R2 897 120	R1 811*
		Network and Internet (30)	2 400	R4 345 680	R1 811
		Infrastructure (30)	2 400	R4 345 680	R1 811
		Security (20)	1 600	R2 897 120	R1 811
			8 000	R14 485 600	R1 811

(*R2 879 120 (from Table 5) × 1 600 h (from Table 3))
Source Compiled by authors from accumulated data

With the total indirect cost calculated, the allocation of the indirect cost could then be allocated to the service departments. Note that, as indicated in the document analysis, the CEO office and Legal Supporting Department did not have a direct trace to specific service department. Thus, they were not allocated to a service (Table 8).

The indirect cost per hour was calculated within each of the service departments, which could then be allocated to the direct object or client.

Table 7 Total indirect cost

	Finance	*HR*	*IT*	*Sales*	*Operations*	*Engineers*	*Project*	*Legal*	*Marketing*	*CEO Office*
Rent (4 000 m^2)										
Capacity	250	70	70	1 400	250	1 300	330	40	250	40
Unit cost	R75	R75	R75	R75	R75	R75	R75	R75	R75	R75
Total	R18 750	R5 250	R5 250	R105 000	R18 750	R97 500	R24 750	R3 000	R18 750	R3 000
Water and electricity (15 000kw)										
Capacity	900	150	150	5 400	900	5 200	1 200	100	900	100
Unit cost	R2	R2	R2	R2	R2	R2	R2	R2	R2	R2
Total	R1 800	R300	R300	R10 800	R1 800	R10 400	R2 400	R200	R1 800	R200
Computer depreciation (300 units)										
Capacity	25	6	4	100	20	96	25	2	20	2
Unit cost	R15 000	R15 000	R15 000	R15 000	R15 000	R15 000	R15 000	R15 000	R15 000	R15 000
Total	R375 000	R90 000	R60 000	R1 500 000	R300 000	R1 440 000	R375 000	R30 000	R300 000	R30 000
Supporting department (direct labour)										
	R5 948 082	R2 167 288	R0	R0	R0	R0	R3 106 208	R297 467	R3 259 333	R811 067
Total indirect cost (R20 419 445)										
	R6 343 632	R2 262 838	R65 550	R1 615 800	R320 550	R1 547 900	R3 508 358	R330 667	R3 579 883	R844 267

Source Compiled by authors from accumulated data

Table 8 Allocation of indirect cost

		IT	*Sales*	*Operations*	*Engineers*
Finance	R6 343 632	5%	60%	10%	25%
HR	R2 262 838	5%	30%	10%	55%
Project	R3 508 358	10%	30%	20%	40%
Marketing	R3 579 883	5%	70%	15%	10%
Finance	R6 343 632	R317 182	R3 806 179	R634 363	R1 585 908
HR	R2 262 838	R113 142	R678 851	R226 284	R1 244 560
Project	R3 508 358	R350 835	R1 052 508	R701 671	R1 403 343
Marketing	R3 579 883	R178 994	R125 296	R18 794	R1 879
Total	R15 694 711	R960 154	R5 662 834	R1581 113	R4 235 691
Indirect cost		R65 550	R1 615 800	R320 550	R1 547 900
Total indirect cost		R1 025 704	R7 278 634	R1 901 663	R5 793 591
Total capacity hrs/month		666.67*	16 000	3 333.33	13 666.67
Cost per hour		R1 538.56**	R454.91	R570.50	R423.19

(*8 000 (from Table 6)/12 months; **R1 025 704/666.67)
Source Compiled by authors from accumulated data

7.3 *Evaluation*

The evaluation phase was included the artefact practical example in order to illustrate and be evaluated against a potential client for Firm A. As a result, the costing system will help Firm A to ensure that there is sufficient capacity in each department/activity so as to accept the potential client's offer. The system will also cost the client's request for the use of Firm's A services. The following is an example to explain this costing system: Client X approaches Firm A to implement/use their services and resources. The following questions should be answered:

- What activities are going to be used?
- How many hours per month are going to be used in each activity requested?

Client X should answer these questions via their request for a quote from Firm A. Thus, Firm A can calculate the cost of activities (and their usage) and can also ensure that the firm does have sufficient capacity to accept the request.

For the purposes of the example, it is supposed that Client X sent the following activities and hours that they requested to make use of each month:

- Service sales (Sales) = **2** hours
- Client management (Sales) = **3** hours
- Smart Solutions (IT) = **90** hours
- Network and internet (IT) = **90** hours
- Deliverables (Operations) = **10** hours
- Strategic planning (Operations) = **5** hours
- Deliverables (Product Engineer) = **50** hours
- Project Drafts (Product Engineer) = **25** hours
- Total hours = **275** hours

Thus, if Firm A has sufficient capacity in each activity, it may accept the offer and commence calculating the cost. If not, Firm A could still accept the offer, but its employees might then have to work over-time, or the firm could outsource the activities that are over and above its capacity.

Working from the assumption that Firm A has sufficient capacity and decides to deliver the service to Client X (Table 9).

Thus, Client X will be charged R719 374,10 per month for providing 275 hours' service. As a result, the cost of R719 374,10 would be the minimum value that Firm A would accept.

8 Conclusion

Within the context of the systems theory, this study investigated the current costing model of the case study principle in order to establish a reliable system that would improve cost allocation and provide data for

Table 9 Costing—Client X

Activity	*Hours*	*Direct labour rate*	*Indirect labour rate*	*Total rate*	*Total cost*
Service sales	2	R668	R455	R1 123	R2 246
Client management	3	R537	R455	R991	R2 976
Smart solutions	90	R1 811	R1 539	R3 349	R301 460
Network and internet	90	R1 811	R1 539	R3 349	R301 460
Deliverables	10	R1 007	R570	R1 577	R15 775
Strategic planning	5	R2 433	R570	R3 003	R15 017
Deliverables	50	R693	R423	R1 116	R55 809
Project drafts	25	R562	R423	R985	R24 630
Total	275				R719 374

Source Compiled by authors from accumulated data

informed decision-making in an effort to maximise value and to remain relevant in the market.

The authors found that Firm A does not have a trustworthy costing system when quotations are given to clients. Firm A currently does not cost their customer service, installation teams, project management teams and revisits. By applying ADR, the authors used the inductive approach to develop a new costing system for Firm A, based on the TDABC approach. In conclusion, the new costing system is desirable for Firm A to quote their clients more accurately and eliminate cross-subsidy.

The recommendation is that Firm A should implement the new costing system as a starting point and then adapt/change/integrate/improve the costing system, as the model in this study is only an example. The rand values were approximately 80% accurate and the working hours were a calculated estimated value.

In the context of the systems theory, which states that one should understand the ways and purpose of a system in order to understand the process as a whole, the contribution of the study is explained as follows.

Following the Hutchins (1996) framework, the systems theory was divided into the following four components:

- Firstly, *the description of the aspects/nature of the specific system*—the nature of the costing system is a TDABC system that is time-based, allowing Firm A to integrate the costing system with their ERP system. Consequently, the costing system could be updated automatically through the ERP system, which would equip them with a quicker response towards the costing system;

- Secondly, *the explanation of how the components in the system interact*—the components in the systems are based on TDABC, where time is the main overhead activity driver. The time is allocated to the different departments and activities and then to the different management level(s). The management level cost driver is multiplied with the specific times, enabling the system to cost the activities;
- Thirdly, *the determination whether the system is effective*—the costing system that was developed for Firm A was evaluated against an artefact practical example. This would illustrate how the costing system works and whether it is adequate for Firm A to implement it in its costing processes and
- Fourthly, *the identification of the extent which the systems can function in practice compared to the ideal jointed use of archival material*—this costing system is functional in the (in)direct labour hours system since Firm A is a digital technology service firm, providing mostly labour hours (time) to its clients.

References

Accenture. 2019. *The post-digital era is upon us. Are you ready for what's next?* https://www.accenture.com/_acnmedia/pdf-108/accenture-communications-technology-vision-2019-full-report.pdf. Date of accessed 12 January 2020.

Aguilar, O.I., and C.D. Ittner. 2018. Cost management in the digital era. *China Management Review* 4 (2): 14–21.

Bhimani, A., and M. Bromwich. 2009. *Management accounting in a digital and global economy: The interface of strategy, technology, and cost information*. London: Oxford University Press.

Bvumbi, M.N. 2017. *An analysis of the implementation of activity based costing at the Water Trading Entity* (Dissertation – MPhil). Pretoria: UNISA.

Chea, A.C. 2011. Activity-based costing system in the service sector: a strategic approach for enhancing managerial decision making and competitiveness. *International Journal of Business and Management* 6 (11): 3–10.

CIMA. 2013. *Activity-Based Costing (ABC)*. https://www.cgma.org/resources/tools/essential-tools/activity-based-costing.html. Date of accessed 5 February 2020.

CIMA. 2019. *Re-inventing finance for a digital world*. https://www.cimaglobal.com/Future/the-future-of-finance/. Date of accessed 5 February 2020.

Deloitte. 2019. *Save-to-transform as a catalyst for embracing digital disruption*. https://www2.deloitte.com/us/en/pages/operations/articles/global-cost-management-survey.html. Date of accessed 27 February 2020.

Drury, C. 2012. *Management and cost accounting*, 8th ed. Andover: Cengage Learning.

Gunasekaran, A., H.J. Williams, and R.E. MacGaughey. 2005. Performance measurement and costing system in a new enterprise. *Technovation* 25: 523–533.

Hevner, A., S. March, J. Park, and S. Ram. 2004. Design science in information systems research. *MIS Quarterly* 28 (1): 75–105.

Hutchins, L.C. 1996. *Systems thinking: Solving complex problems*. Saint Louis, MO: Professional Development Systems.

IDC (International Data Corporation). 2018. *Worldwide spending on digital transformation will reach $2.3 Trillion in 2023*. https://www.idc.com/getdoc.jsp?containerId=prUS45612419. Date of accessed 24 November 2019.

Jan, O. 2013. *Cost accounting systems*. https://xplaind.com/360325/cost-systems. Date of accessed 10 April 2020.

Johnson, H.T., and R.S. Kaplan. 1987. *Relevance lost: The rise and fall of management accounting*. Boston: Harvard Business School Press.

Kaplan, R.S., and S.R. Anderson. 2007. *Time-driven activity-based costing*. Boston: Harvard Business School Press.

Kessler, E.H. 2017. *Encyclopaedia of management theory*. London: Sage.

Maluleke, M.J. 2019. *Comparative analysis of activity based costing as an alternative to the traditional costing methods in SASSA* (Thesis – MPhil). Pretoria: UNISA.

Mullarkey, M.T., and A.R. Hevner. 2019. An elaborated action design research process model. *European Journal of Information Systems* 28 (1): 6–20.

Ngcobo, N.L. 2019. *An evaluation of an activity-driven operational cost accounting framework in an electricity distribution company* (Mini-dissertation – MCom). Potchefstroom: North-West University.

Nkuna, M.R. 2018. *Developing an activity-driven costing framework for a South African cash service company* (Mini-dissertation – MCom). Potchefstroom: North-West University.

Popesko, B. 2009. How to implement an accurate and effective costing system in manufacturing organizations. *European Financial and Accounting Journal* 4 (4): 35–49.

Stouthuysen, K., K. Schierhout, F. Roodhooft, and E. Reusen. 2014. Time-driven activity-based costing for public services. *Public Money & Management* 34 (4): 289–296.

Szychta, A. 2010. Time-driven activity-based costing in service industries. *Social Sciences* 1 (67): 49–60.

Teece, D. 2018. Dynamic capabilities as (workable) management systems theory. *Journal of Management & Organization* 24 (3): 359–368.

Tilo, N.L. 2017. *The role of management accountants to facilitate sustainable business success in big Lesotho companies* (Dissertation – MCom). Potchefstroom: North-West University.

Van der Linde, M. 2011. *Embedding an activity driven operational accounting framework in a fertilizer* (Mini-dissertation – MCom). Potchefstroom: North-West University.

CHAPTER 5

Designing a Cost Management Framework for a Medical Scheme Service Provider in South Africa

Elbie Ward, Susanna L Middelberg, and Pieter Buys

Abstract The South African medical scheme environment is heavily regulated. Furthermore, healthcare costs are continuously on the rise, requiring medical schemes to be creative in managing their costs while offering quality healthcare. One of the innovative ways to manage costs, is channelling its members towards a cost-efficient, high quality medical specialist's network. This case study focuses on the development of a framework that is able to detect and recommend the most cost-effective route in identifying quality medical specialists and channelling members thereto. The results illustrate that channelling members to cost-efficient, quality medical specialists can lead to substantial cost savings for the

E. Ward · S. L. Middelberg (✉) · P. Buys
Management Cybernetics Research Entity, North-West University, Potchefstroom, South Africa
e-mail: sanlie.middelberg@nwu.ac.za

P. Buys
e-mail: pieter.buys@nwu.ac.za

P. Buys (ed.), *Designing Cost Management Systems to Support Business Decision-Making*, https://doi.org/10.1007/978-981-16-1751-5_5

medical scheme. Through the involvement of key stakeholders, a solution was found to the problem of increasing medical costs to the benefit of all.

Keywords Cost management · Healthcare service providers · Medical costs · Service provider networks

JEL Classification I13 (Health insurance) · I18 (Government policy · public health) · M41 (Accounting)

1 Introduction

Worldwide, healthcare costs are on the rise (WHO 2019) and in South Africa this is no exception. Healthcare inflation is year-on-year higher than the Consumer Price Index (Erasmus and Fourie 2014; Warburton 2019). There are several reasons for the rise in healthcare costs. Although medical innovation is essential in improving the quality of life as well as lifespan, medical innovation can be expensive (Custer 2016). It is expensive not only due to the cost of new technologies and pharmaceuticals, but also a longer life expectation. The more elderly people within a population, the higher the chronic diseases and co-morbidities and therefore medical bills. This in turn leads to an increase in the average age of insured members as well as an increase in disease financial burden. Hospital costs are continuously increasing, with high annual increases and more beds that are being filled. Venter et al. (2013) also describe staff shortages, which lead to longer working hours and longer waiting periods for consultations and procedures. This makes for a high demand and therefore many healthcare practitioners can adjust their fees to their liking.

The South African Medical Schemes Act (MSA), stipulates that prescribed minimum benefit (PMB) conditions should be paid in full, which are defined by the Council for Medical Schemes (CMS 2011). This set of benefits ensures that all medical scheme members can access certain minimum basic healthcare services, regardless of the benefit of the option they have selected. The aim is to provide people with continuous medical care to improve their health and well-being and to make such medical care more affordable. However, without a fixed price reference, the use of PMB conditions has led to abuse by some healthcare practitioners with absorbent claims for PMB treatments (CCSA 2018).

One of the (legal) innovative ways to curb these rising medical costs, is for medical schemes to form designated service provider (DSP) networks. These DSPs are the healthcare practitioners, related service providers and hospitals which have entered into agreements with medical schemes to make their services available at a negotiated price (CMS 2011). These networks are typically all-inclusive to ensure easy access for members. On the down-side however, it may mean that DSP networks find themselves keeping low-quality healthcare practitioners on the network for the sake of broad access.

With this in mind, medical schemes have to be creative in how they channel members to high quality healthcare service providers (in this case study certain medical specialists were used), while remaining cost-efficient. Network channelling is often done through financial incentives. Positive incentives include receiving some kind of gift, reward or free service, while negative incentives come in the form of financial penalties or co-payments. Positive incentives are not allowed for self-administered schemes under the MSA, while negative incentives may lead to reputational damage. Other methods include advice or referrals. This can be done by either a medical scheme's call centre, or a general practitioner (GP) referring a patient to a medical specialist. GPs choose at least 43% of specialists when referring members. GPs are generally the first point of entry into the private healthcare system and therefore ideal to channel members towards specific, tiered specialists. (Potappel et al. 2019).

Medical schemes measure the cost efficiency and quality outcomes of the healthcare practitioners through provider profiling and benchmarking. Medical specialists can be profiled and ranked based on medical claims data detailing length of hospital stay, theatre time, re-admission and other indicators. Previous research has been conducted on the use of negative financial incentives' effectiveness in channelling members towards specific healthcare providers and/or tiered networks in the Netherlands (Bes et al. 2017), and in the USA (Kyanko et al. 2013; Scanlon et al. 2008; Sinaiko 2011), while Scholle et al. (2008) reported on provider benchmarking and the reliability of measures used in the USA. Other successful ways of channelling members towards certain providers were reported by Bes et al. (2018) in the Netherlands. However, there is a lack of research on using network channelling by medical schemes through referrals by

GPs to minimise cost without compromising quality, especially in a South African context.

The aim of this case study is to develop a framework that can identify and recommend the most cost-effective route in identifying quality medical specialists and channelling members thereto. This study contributes value to the industry by providing a guideline on how to evaluate and display information on the cost-effectiveness of medical specialists and how to present these for optimal channelling with the best outcomes. This will assist medical schemes in managing healthcare cost while still ensuring members receive the best quality care.

2 Literature Study

Medical schemes function as an intermediary between its members and healthcare service providers. To grow their membership base, schemes need to offer benefit options with an attractive network of healthcare providers at an affordable rate (Bes et al. 2017). Although it may naturally be assumed that medical schemes with a larger market share would be in a better position, a scheme's ability to channel members to preferred providers or DSPs is even more important (Bes et al. 2017; Sorensen 2003; Wu 2009). Prior research conducted on network channelling include Sinaiko (2011), who conducted a survey in the USA to test the relationship between negative financial incentives and tiered network channelling. Sinaiko (2011) found that tiering (or rating according to cost impact and profiling) had the biggest impact when members were looking for a new healthcare provider. Sinaiko (2011) posited that by using profiling tools, thus allowing for providers to be ranked within a network, creating a tiered network. This relationship between negative financial incentives and tiered networks was also confirmed by Kyanko et al. (2013). The results indicated that in an effective, established network where negative financial incentives apply, most patients will visit in-network providers. Within a tiered network, members have freedom concerning the choice of a healthcare service provider. The healthcare service providers were ranked by their medical scheme on the scheme's level of preference, i.e. based on their performance on cost-effectiveness and service quality.

Other successful ways of channelling members towards certain healthcare providers entail offering advice on their choice of medical specialist when they phone the medical scheme's contact centre. A study by Bes et al. (2018) in the Netherlands, concluded that although channelling may be successful, it could not be confirmed whether a relationship was formed between the healthcare service provider and the member. A similar study by Scanlon et al. (2008), found that the more senior, *educated* members had more visits to the higher tiered hospitals, which indicates that such members better understand the value and incentives of making use of a higher tiered hospital.

Provider benchmarking and the reliability of the performance measures were reported on by Scholle et al. (2008). Administrative data were used from nine health plans to evaluate the performance of healthcare providers using certain performance measures. Even though this study was completed more than a decade ago, the emphasis on the quality and reliability of the measures cannot be ignored. From this study it was evident that profiling healthcare providers offers an excellent base to build ranked or tiered networks.

From the above it is evident that network channelling and benchmarking healthcare providers based on cost impact and quality of service are acceptable practice. There is however a lack of research on South African medical schemes utilising network channelling and provider healthcare service provider profiling with the aim of curbing the increasing healthcare costs. This case study aims to address this knowledge gap.

3 Theoretical and Conceptual Framework

Rising healthcare costs negatively influence all stakeholders, including medical scheme members, healthcare providers and medical scheme service providers. The channelling framework in this case study was designed with the aim to benefit the healthcare service provider (through more referrals), the medical scheme member (by receiving treatment from healthcare services providers identified as providing high quality, cost-effective services) and the medical scheme (through channelling members towards cost-effective providers and therefore managing costs).

Stakeholder theory was put forward by Freeman (1984), in which it is argued that individuals or groups with legitimate interests partake in organisations to obtain benefits. There is however, no precedence of one set of interests and benefits over another (Smith 2003). Whether priorities are aligned or not, all stakeholders should derive a benefit and expectations should be met. Stakeholder theory is commonly applied in a business context and integrating stakeholder and organisational interest is the focus of stakeholder theory (Filipovic et al. 2010). Stakeholders can be viewed as those affected by, and/or can influence the achievement of, an organisation's business objectives (Freeman 1984), which should entail the creation of value for all stakeholders involved (Freeman etal. 2010). This case study focused on finding a solution to the problem of rising healthcare costs, which should benefit all pertinent stakeholders including the members, the service providers and medical scheme itself.

The conceptual framework of this study posited that provider profiling can be used to rank healthcare service providers, and should medical schemes be able to channel members towards the higher-ranked medical specialists using the provider profiling, it could assist with cost containment. Figure 1 shows an overview of the research problem and conceptual framework.

With the ever-rising healthcare cost at the centre of the research problem, medical schemes have to attempt to channel members towards the higher ranked, lower cost impact providers. High quality outcomes are directly linked to cost efficiencies, including a shorter hospital stay, often shorter theatre times and less re-admissions. One would therefore prefer the members to consult with lower cost impact (or higher cost-efficient) providers, shown by the dotted line in Fig. 1, rather than providers with a higher cost impact, in an attempt to manage hospital and procedural costs.

Taking cognisance of the stakeholder theoretical framework, a cost management framework was designed to channel members to cost-efficient providers.

4 Research Design

An action design research (ADR) approach was followed utilising a mixed methods research strategy in a single South African based medical scheme, i.e. a case study. ADR is a research approach that generates knowledge through the collaborative creation and evaluation of artefacts in an organisation (Sein et al. 2011). ADR can be used effectively in numerous research projects and, with its ever-expanding applications, the ADR process continues to evolve in an attempt to address the needs of changing and challenging environments (Mullarkey and Hevner 2018), such as the medical scheme industry. Figure 2 provides an overview of the four ADR stages and possible entry points.

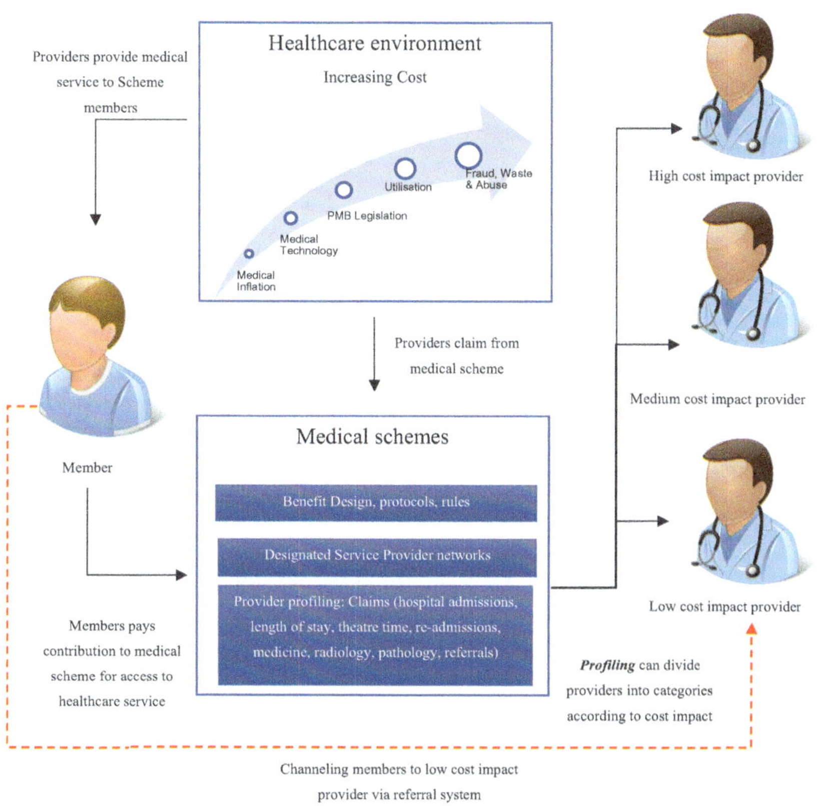

Fig. 1 Overview of the research problem and conceptual framework

Figure 2 shows a summary of the four stages of ADR and possible entry points. The diagnosis phase was the entry point into this case study. This is well-supported by the literature, as Mullarkey and Hevner (2018) argue ADR to be most effective at the earliest entry point and Sein and Rossi (2019) view the diagnosis (problem formulation) phase as the only real entry point into ADR.

The diagnosis phase attempted to test the concept of cost management through member channelling to ranked healthcare service providers. The research was conducted through an analysis of secondary quantitative data on actual, existing, primary medical claims data of the medical scheme

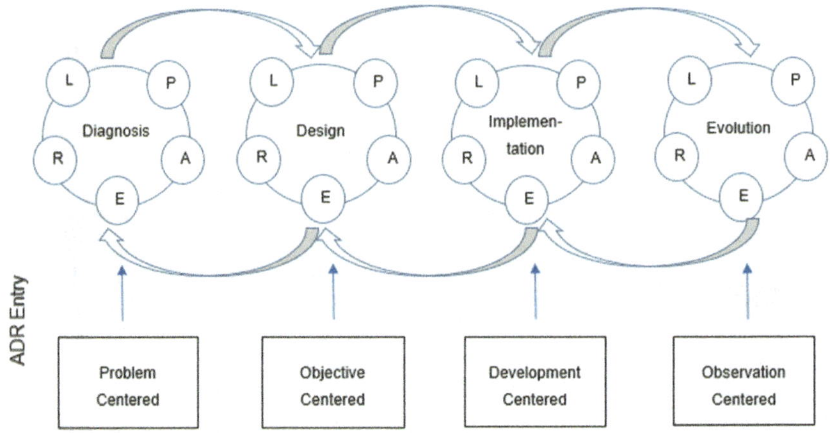

Fig. 2 The four ADR stages and possible entry points (*Source* Mullarkey and Hevner 2018)

of close to 200,000 medical scheme beneficiaries. This quantitative data was supported by qualitative data gathered through semi-structured interviews with key stakeholders, including actuaries, doctors and scheme managers. Medical procedures to be included were selected for the data analysis based on (i) the consistency in the way procedures are performed, (ii) the volume of procedures available and (iii) the cost impact the procedure may have. Three medical procedures selected, that being:

- Cataract surgeries, performed by ophthalmologists;
- Caesarean sections, performed by gynaecologists and
- Hip replacements performed by orthopaedic surgeons.

The research was conducted in three phases. In designing the framework, the possibility of using network channelling to medical specialists as a way of managing cost was initially conceptually tested using historical claims data (Phase 1). Following the proof of concept, an *Alpha*-design framework (in a pdf format) was tested and piloted with a sample of general medical practitioners (GP). The feedback from the pilot of the *Alpha*-design was used to build, implement and evaluate an improved, digital artefact in the second *Beta*-design framework (Phase 3).

5 Results

The results are presented based on the three phases of the research described above.

5.1 *Phase 1: Proof of Concept*

Phase 1 comprised that historical member claims data from the case study organisation were cleaned and outliers removed. Thereafter, based on 12 months of data, an assumption was made that if a more efficient medical specialist was available within the same hospital where the member received the procedure (i.e. cataract surgery, caesarean section or hip replacement), channelling would have been possible, but no inter-hospital channelling would have occurred. If a specific medical specialist used was the most cost-effective provider, the assumption was made that the member would have stayed at that provider. If a specific medical specialist was the only one available within the hospital/facility, it was assumed the member would have stayed at the medical specialist for the procedure. By applying this principle, the following 'theoretical' possible cost savings could have been achieved for the three selected procedures:

- Cataract surgery: R553,687[1] or 1.43% of total cost (Pre-channelling total actual costs of 1,504 procedures R38,671,152 less post-theoretical channelling total calculated costs of 1,504 procedures with 270 channelled to higher-ranked ophthalmologists R38,137,465);
- Caesarean section: R2,990,629 or 4.17% of total cost (Pre-channelling total actual costs of 1,702 procedures R71,660,333 less post-theoretical channelling total calculated costs of 1,702 procedures with 757 channelled to higher-ranked gynaecologists R68,669,704);
- Hip replacement surgery: R627,579 or 1.66% of total cost (Pre-channelling total actual costs of 268 procedures R37,820,638 less post-theoretical channelling total calculated costs of 268 procedures with 50 channelled to higher-ranked orthopaedic surgeons R37,193,059).

[1] 'R' refers to the South African Rand, which is the local currency.

A combined estimated saving for the three procedures totalled R4,171,895 or 2.8% of the total cost. These possible cost savings were substantial in monetary terms and were accepted as proof of concept to enter the design phases (Phases 2 and 3).

5.2 *Phase 2:* Alpha-*Design*

The outcome of the second phase was the *Alpha*-design framework, which was built in the form of a portable document format (pdf) and tested at a sample of GP practices. The pdf document listed the medical specialists from the highest ranked (most cost-efficient) provider to the lowest ranked specialist. This pdf list was distributed via email and hard copies to 5,258 GPs. GP referrals were used to channel medical scheme members towards the cost-effective medical specialist. As mentioned earlier, GPs are often the point of entry into the private healthcare system and therefore ideal if medical schemes want to channel members towards specific, ranked medical specialists.

In the pdf document, specialists were ranked according to their practice profile, which is based on national benchmarking norms between their peers. The ranked specialists were divided into three groups:

- Group 1: those with a cost impact score of < 0%—the most efficient group,
- Group 2: those with a cost impact score of 0% < 15%,
- Group 3: those with a cost impact score of $\geq$ 15%.

The cost impact score is derived from the cost per admission and admission rate combined into one score and the interpretation of it is illustrated in Fig. 3.

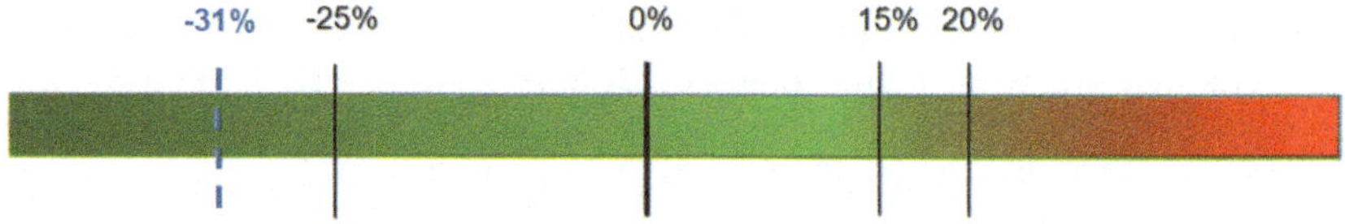

Fig. 3 Cost impact score interpretation

This figure is not according to scale and is for illustration purposes only. As mentioned above, the cost impact score is compiled by the components that form part of the cost per admission and the admission rate with both equally contributing to the cost impact score. A score of 0% shows a cost impact exactly on the norm/benchmark. If a medical specialist has an impact score of 0%, he/she has the same cost impact as the average medical specialist. A cost impact score of below 0% shows a cost impact below the norm. This means the specialist is more cost-effective than his/her peers. A cost impact above 0% implicates the specialist has a higher cost impact than his/her peers and is therefore viewed as less cost-effective. The scheme views a cost impact score of less than 15% as acceptable practice.

An analysis which included the number and percentage of referrals to specialists within each group, was also conducted. The referrals are measured through the number of referred specialist consultations. Since the scheme does not have rules in place that requires a referral from a GP before a member can visit a specialist. Therefore, specialist visits without referrals from GPs are possible. The results of the framework (artefact) implemented in the *Alpha*-design phase is shown in Table 1 below. The percentage each group (Groups 1 to 3) represents of the total procedures are indicated in brackets.

Table 1 indicates that there were less procedures done during the second half of the year concerning all of the three procedures, with cataract surgery at 1,206 vs 793, caesarean sections at 469 vs 352 and hip replacements at 145 vs 117 in the first vs the last six months of 2018. Due to the lower number of procedures, the referrals were less. The actual channelling results (channelling difference), shown in Table 1 after the pdf referral list (artefact) was implemented, show an excellent referral channelling result to the highest ranked specialists (Group 1: cost impact < 0%) for hip replacement surgery (+8%), while cataracts showed a 4% improvement and caesarean sections the lowest improvement with 3% referrals to medical specialists with a cost impact score of less than 0%. A possible explanation could be that women build a relationship with their gynaecologist through regular follow-up visits and are less likely to change to another gynaecologist based on a GP recommendation than for the other disciplines (cataract surgeries and hip replacements).

To calculate the actual cost saving from the network channelling efforts during the α-design phase, the average cost of the procedure was calculated using the actual cost for the procedures before implementation of

Table 1 Channelling number and percentage changes: *Alpha*-design phase

Procedure	*Channelling pre-artefact implementation: January to June 2018*	*Channelling post artefact implementation: July to December 2018*	*Channelling difference*
Cataract surgery	Group 1: 943 (78%) Group 2: 228 (19%) Group 3: 35 (3%) Total: 1,206 Average cost: R26,245.85	Group 1: 648 (82%) Group 2: 137 (17%) Group 3: 8 (1%) Total: 793 Average cost: R24,596.11	Group 1: **+4%** Group 2: −2% Group 3: −2% Saving: **R1,649.75** × 793 = Total savings: **R1,308,248.93**
Caesarean section	Group 1: 264 (56%) Group 2: 148 (32%) Group 3: 57 (12%) Total: 469 Average cost: R43,448.02	Group 1: 207 (59%) Group 2: 103 (29%) Group 3: 42 (12%) Total: 352 Average cost: R42,566.42	Group 1: **+3%** Group 2: −3% Group 3: 0% Saving: **R881.60** × 352 = Total savings: **R310,324.26**
Hip replacement surgery	Group 1: 93 (64%) Group 2: 34 (23%) Group 3: 18 (12%) Total: 145 Average cost: R154,606.99	Group 1: 84 (72%) Group 2: 24 (21%) Group 3: 9 (8%) Total: 117 Average cost: R137,449.32	Group 1: **+8%** Group 2: −4% Group 3: −4% Saving: **R17,157.67** × 117 Total savings: **R2,007,447.19**

the pdf referral list divided by the number of procedures. In all three selected procedures, the average cost reduced indicating that the higher-ranked medical specialists have a lower cost impact. The cost saving per procedure of R1,650, R882 and R17,158, respectively was multiplied by the actual procedures performed during July to December 2018 to establish the cost saving of the medical scheme achieved due to the channelling efforts of members to the highest ranked specialists. A combined cost saving of R3,626,020 was achieved or R1,308,249 by the cataract surgeries, R310,324 by the caesarean sections and R2,007,447 by the hip replacement surgeries.

5.3 *Phase 3:* Beta-*Design*

After the implementation of the pdf referral list, feedback from the GP practices was collated. The feedback received on the pdf referral list from both the GPs and the medical scheme's management indicated that although easy to compile and distribute through a bulk e-mailing system, some shortcomings in the pdf referral list were identified. The pdf framework contained all the information required for the referrals to higher ranked, more cost-effective medical specialists, however, as GPs were not aware of the rationale behind the display (ranking) of specialists, they found it difficult to navigate. The medical scheme also updates the list on a daily basis, which makes it difficult to maintain updated lists at the GP practices.

The feedback received on the *Alpha*-design stage were used to build, implement and evaluate a digital framework in the *Beta*-design stage which represented Phase 3. This framework was converted from a pdf referral list to a digital list (the iCanRefer™ application) and made available to GPs on their practice management system. Due to the significant cost of rolling out the solution, a small sample of 20 GPs were selected to test the framework. The digital framework enabled GPs to search for a medical specialist in their area, on their in-house practice management system. The results would display the medical specialists in the area, per discipline, and would show in ranked order. The ease of use of the newly developed digital framework promoted the usage of the referral application. This was clearly displayed through the results: referrals to higher-ranked specialists (Group 1) increased from 32 to 84% of all specialist referrals. The results are presented in Fig. 4.

The iCanRefer™ application was implemented in January 2019. Figure 4 shows the different values for the pilot group during July to December 2018 compared to January to June 2019. For the pilot group, there were 462 more consultations at the GP practice during January to June 2019 than during July to December 2018. The referral percentage, i.e. the number of consultations that were referred, changed from 12 to 13% resulting in 240 v 320 referrals to medical specialists for any reason or procedure during the two time periods. According to actual medical scheme data, roughly 38% of all referrals from GPs to medical specialists results in hospital procedures. If this is calculated over a 12-month period using the combined total of the referrals for both periods (240 + 320) and multiplied by roughly 38%, the result is 215 procedures. The actual

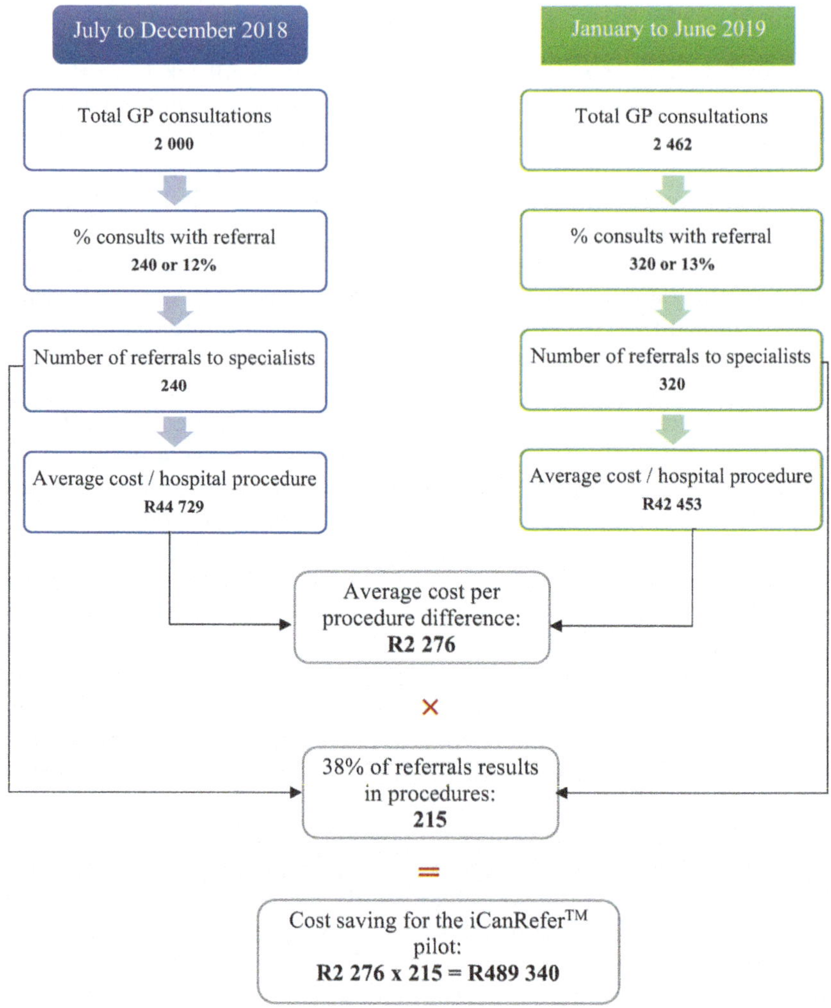

Fig. 4 Cost impact of the digital framework on the pilot group

average cost per case changed from R44,729 during the first six months, to R42,453 in the next six months. As the period runs over a year-end (31 December 2018), adjustments were made by the actuaries—contracted by the Scheme as independent consultants—for a CPI increase. This shows an average decrease of R2,276 per procedure due to more referrals to the Group 1, i.e. the most cost-effective, specialists. The average saving per procedure was applied across the medical scheme to predict a potential impact if the iCanRefer™ application is rolled out to all network GPs. The estimated saving is shown in Fig. 5.

Figure 5 shows the estimated cost saving for the medical scheme if the same average cost per referred procedure applies across all referred hospital procedures and not only to the sample three procedures of cataract surgeries, caesarean sections and hip replacements. In total, there were 321,092 GP consultations over the same 12-month period of July 2018 to June 2019. Of the 321,092, 14% (44,953) were referred. The principle (based on the actual medical scheme claims data) that around 38% of all referrals from a GP to a specialist will result in a hospital procedure, was applied. This resulted in 17,082 referred procedures. If the cost difference of R2,276, as explained in the discussion of Fig. 4, is applied, this may result in an annual saving of R38,878,632.

6 Discussion and Conclusion

The aim of this study was to develop a framework able to identify and recommend the most cost-effective route in identifying appropriate medical specialists and channelling members thereto. This was in response to the problem of increasing healthcare costs. The research was conducted using an ADR approach, which was applied in a medical scheme service provider, comprising a conceptual phase and two design phases.

- The first, conceptual phase (or proof of concept) evaluated historical member claims data over a 12-month period by applying a theoretical channelling principle. It was assumed that members may be channelled to a higher-ranked medical specialist if one was available within the same facility as where they had the procedure. For the three procedures, this could have resulted in a saving of R4,171,895 over the 12 months. This potential savings justified further research and development into the envisaged cost management framework.

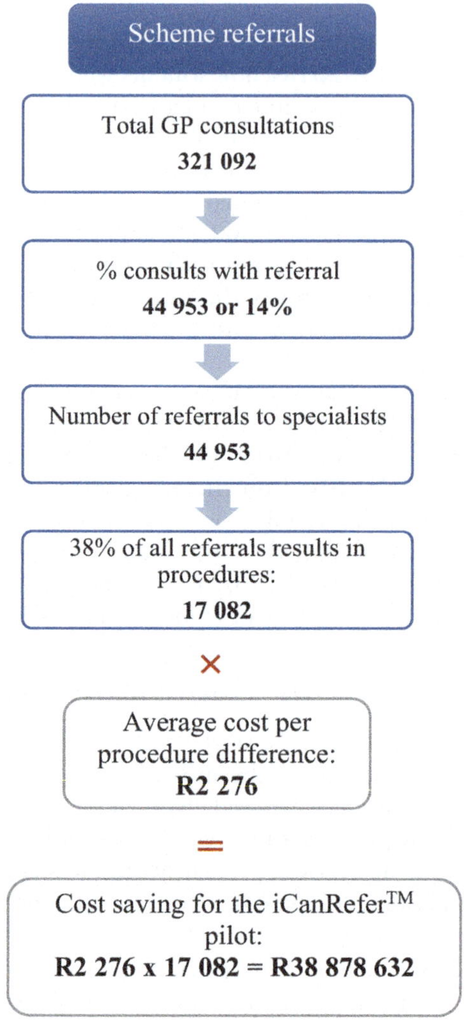

Fig. 5 Potential cost impact of digital framework on the Scheme

- The results from the second, or *Alpha*-design phase were based on actual referrals (member channelling) through the implementation of the pdf referral lists at GP practices. The referral changes to higher-ranked medical specialists resulted in an actual saving of R3,626,020. When applying these cost savings across all procedure

cost for the Scheme, and if the same assumptions are applied, could lead to a potential cost saving of R48,793,633.
- The evaluation of the results of the digital artefact in the third, *Beta*-design phase were based on actual referral data of a sample size of 20 GPs, which indicated an estimated saving of R489,340. These savings were then also extrapolated across all procedure cost for the Scheme, which could lead to further saving of R38,878,632.

This case study emphasises the possibility of using networks, and a referral framework that promotes the use of higher-ranked, cost-effective medical specialists as a contributor to managing medical expenditure. It is recommended that this should be expanded to all disciplines and all procedures in the medical scheme, and not only the three selected procedures of cataract surgery, caesarean section and hip replacement surgery. Furthermore, a digital artefact on the practice management system, where GPs and specialists do not have to leave their working page and login to a separate site to search for a medical specialist, will promote the best use of the application and ranked specialists.

The limitations of the study include that only three procedures were selected based on the criteria described in the research design. Although care was taken and stakeholder input gathered to validate the selection, the three procedures may not represent all procedures across all disciplines.

The case study illustrated that being cognisant of the requirements of key stakeholders (i.e. the specialists, GPs, scheme, members and application developers in this instance) contributes substantially in ensuring the design of an effective cost management framework. The medical specialists benefitted through more referrals, the GPs by ensuring the route to refer within the DSP is easily accessible and user-friendly, the members by gaining access to high quality, cost-effective medical specialists and the application providers through increased revenue. This could be achieved as follows:

- Firstly, the framework incorporates the key stakeholder requirements;
- Secondly, due to the aforementioned the testing and implementation processes was completed with minimum effort and

- Thirdly, the information generated within the framework provides relevant business decision-making support and addresses the research problem.

The study contributes to the industry by providing a design process other medical schemes could follow in developing a network channelling framework that can benefit all stakeholders and address the problem of escalating healthcare costs.

References

Bes, R.E., E.C. Curfs, P.P. Groenewegen, and J.D. De Jong. 2017. Selective contracting and channelling patients to preferred providers: A scoping review. *Health Policy* 121 (5): 504–514.

Bes, R.E., E.C. Curfs, P.P. Groenewegen, and J.D. De Jong. 2018. Advice from the health insurer as a channelling strategy: A natural experiment at a Dutch health insurance company. *BMC Health Services Research* 18 (1): Art. 832.

CCSA (Competition Commission South Africa). 2018. *Health market inquiry: Provisional findings and recommendations report*. Pretoria: CCSA.

CMS (Council for Medical Schemes). 2011. The ABC of PMBs. cmscript, 7 of 2010–2011.

Custer, W. 2016. Health care cost inflation in the next decade. *Journal of Financial Service Professionals* 70 (1): 37–39.

Erasmus, M., and H. Fourie. 2014. *Rising prices in the healthcare sector: unpacking health inflation*. http://econex.co.za/wp-content/uploads/2015/03/econex_researchnote_36.pdf. Date of access: 10 March 2017.

Filipovic, D., N. Podrug, and M. Kristo. 2010. Assessment of relations between stewardship and stakeholder theory. *Annals of DAAAM & Proceedings* 21 (1): 1229–1230.

Freeman, R.E. 1984. *Strategic management: A stakeholder approach*. Cambridge: Cambridge University Press.

Freeman, R.E., J.S. Harrison, A.C. Wicks, B.L. Parmar, and S. de Colle. 2010. *Stakeholder theory: The state of the art*. Cambridge: Cambridge University Press.

Kyanko, K.A., L.A. Curry, and S.H. Busch. 2013. Out-of-network physicians: How prevalent are involuntary use and cost transparency? *Health Services Research* 48 (3): 1154–1172.

Mullarkey, M.T., and A.R. Hevner. 2018. An elaborated action design research process model. *European Journal of Information Systems* 28 (1): 6–20.

Potappel, A.J.C., M.C. Meijers, C. Kloek, A. Victoor, J. Noordman, T.O. Hartman, S. Van Dulmen, and J.D. De Jong. 2019. To what degree do patients actively choose their healthcare provider at the point of referral by their GP? A video observation study. *BMC Family Practice* 20 (1): Art. 166.

Scanlon, D.P., R.C. Lindrooth, and J.B. Christianson. 2008. Steering patients to safer hospitals? The effect of a tiered hospital network on hospital admissions. *Health Services Research* 43 (5 pt 2): 1849–1868.

Scholle, S., J. Roski, J. Adams, D. Dunn, E. Kerr, D. Dugan, and R. Jensen. 2008. Benchmarking physician performance: Reliability of individual and composite measures. *The American Journal of Managed Care* 14 (12): 829–838.

Sein, M.K., O. Henfridsson, S. Purao, M. Rossi, and R. Lindgren. 2011. Action design research. *MIS Quarterly* 35 (1): 37–56.

Sein, M.K., and M. Rossi. 2019. Elaborating ADR while drifting away from its essence: A commentary on Mullarkey and Hevner. *European Journal of Information Systems* 28 (1): 21–25.

Sinaiko, A.D. 2011. How do quality information and cost affect patient choice of provider in a tiered network setting? Results from a survey. *Health Services Research* 46 (2): 437–456.

Smith, H.J. 2003. The shareholders vs. Stakeholders debate. *MIT Sloan Management Review* 44 (4): 85–90.

Sorensen, A.T. 2003. Insurer-hospital bargaining: Negotiated discounts in post-deregulation Connecticut. *Journal of Industrial Economics* 51 (4): 469–490.

Venter, F., A. Constantinou, and Z. Brey 2013. *Rising cost in the healthcare sector—Who's to blame?* http://www.dnaeconomics.com/pages/competition_blog/?zDispID=NewsArtRising_costs_in_the_healthcare_sector__whos_to_blame. Date of access: 10 March 2017.

Warburton, L. 2019. Managing the rising costs of healthcare provision. *Taxtalk* 2019: 30–32.

WHO (World Health Organization). 2019. *Global spending in health: A world in transition*. Geneva, Switzerland: WHO (No. WHO/HIS/HGF/HFWorkingPaper/19.4).

Wu, V.Y. 2009. Managed care's price bargaining with hospitals. *Journal of Health Economics* 28 (2): 350–360.

CHAPTER 6

Considerations of Activity-Based Costing in the Public Sector: The Case of SASSA

Mashangu Justice Maluleke and Merwe Oberholzer

Abstract Although South Africans face severe poverty, there is a governmental desire to address it with social security grants. However, the constant increase in beneficiaries directly affects the administration cost associated with the South African Social Security Agency's (SASSA) social security grants system. This case study aimed to investigate activity-based costing (ABC) and activity-based budgeting (ABB) as alternate approaches to SASSA's current costs management approach. The findings suggest that an activity-based management approach be implemented as an alternative method in SASSA on a pilot project basis. Even though the results of the study cannot be generalised, the lessons learnt from this

M. J. Maluleke
University of South Africa, Pretoria, South Africa
e-mail: 31427755@mylifeunisaac.onmicrosoft.com

M. Oberholzer (✉)
Management Cybernetics Research Entity, North-West University, Potchefstroom, South Africa
e-mail: merwe.oberholzer@nwu.ac.za

P. Buys (ed.), *Designing Cost Management Systems to Support Business Decision-Making*, https://doi.org/10.1007/978-981-16-1751-5_6

study may be crucial for prospective public sector ABC-adopters including the factors to be considered for the successful implementation of ABC.

Keywords Activity-based costing · Activity-based budgeting · Activity-based management · Indirect cost · Public sector costing · Social grants

JEL Classifications M41 (Accounting) · L88 (Government Policy) · H41 (Public Goods)

1 Introduction

Even though the South African Constitution strives to create an equal society, the country arguably remains as one of the most unequal (IMF 2020). The South African Government's social assistance programme aims to facilitate the enablement and the awareness of the right to social security. Consequently, there has been a substantial rate of increase in beneficiaries in the social assistance programme. In this context, the South African Social Security Agency (SASSA) is the vehicle within which this programme takes form, as mandated by the Social Security Agency Act (9 of 2004). SASSA in itself, is a public sector entity governed by the Department of Social Development, and administers eight types of grants namely (SASSA 2019):

- Old-age grant;
- Disability grant;
- War veterans' grant;
- Foster child grant;
- Care dependency grant;
- Child support grant;
- Grant-in-aid and
- Social relief of distress grant.

The actual social assistance grants in recent years amounted to around R150.2 billion (2017/18) and R162.7 billion (2018/19), which benefited 31% (nearly 18 million grants) of the country's population.

However, around R7.2 billion (2017/18) and R6.5 billion (2018/19) was required for SASSA to administrate the payment of the social grants (SASSA 2019). This raises the question of cost effectiveness within SASSA. In managing its processes, SASSA currently uses a conventional costing system to allocate the administrative cost for social security grants. In contrast to this practice, Drury (2018) argues that the application of activity-based costing (ABC) principles, i.e. the gauging and reporting of resource consumption in administrative processes, will probably result in more correct cost allocation and related information than that found in more conventional approaches. Related, supportive studies on ABC in the public sector entities include Baird (2007), Bvumbi (2017), Kee (2012), Oseifuah (2014), Stouthuysen et al. (2014), Tuccillo and Agliata (2018) and Priyatmo and Akbar (2019). The results of these studies however, cannot merely be implemented at SASSA, since its structures, processes and systems are unique. Consequently, the key aim of this case study was to consider the feasibility of ABC's, from a holistic integrated systems' thinking perspective, as an alternative to SASSA's current approach.

In doing so, qualitative data were collected from semi-structured interviews with six knowledgeable SASSA employees. Furthermore, from the literature, three research questions were developed and converted into themes to guide the interviews. During the interviews these themes evolved inductively into seven sub-themes (or constructs). The next section provides the background that investigates the relative benefit of using ABC versus conventional costing. Related terms, activity-based budgeting (ABB) and activity-based management (ABM), are also explained. The section thereafter explains the systems and structures of SASSA, which in turn is followed by a literature review that explores conventional costing systems versus ABC in the public sector. The methodology section explains the study design, while the results section provides an analysis of the findings, before the case study findings are summarised and concluded in the final section.

2 Background

2.1 Key Cost Management Concepts

The foundational departure perspective of this case study revolves around the managerial accounting concept of ABC, which is considered as an alternative to conventional volume-based costing approaches. The latter's approach to overhead cost management via a single cost driver allocation rate, is prone to misrepresenting and distorting the actual cost object costs (Johnson and Kaplan 1987; Wang et al. 2010). An important driving force behind the development of ABC is found in the possibility of more accurate and supporting cost information in support of decision-making, which assigns resource costs to cost objects such as products, services or customers, based on the activities performed for the cost objects (Rundora et al. 2013). Therefore, ABC seeks to improve the accuracy of the calculation of a cost object by using the amount of the activity involved in making a product or rendering a service. Therefore, it "keeps a close connection between the activity that drives the cost and the cost itself" (Wachulka-Chan 2019). Even though an ABC approach may reduce some of the limitations of conventional approaches, it arguably has various shortcomings of its own.

ABC is mainly a cost allocation system to assign costs to cost objects and it may have a limited effect on cost control or cost reduction, "since it is always better to control costs at the source and not after the allocation thereof" (Ngcobo 2019). It can supplementary be linked however, to ABM, which is based on the principle that costs are consumed by activities; therefore, proper control of these activities will assure that costs are managed in the long term (Drury 2018). Furthermore, as a budgeting approach ABB builds and expands on the principles of ABC. In focusing on the costs of associated activities required to deliver the applicable goods and services, ABB enhances the sophistication of the operational planning systems (Hansen 2011).

Cardos and Pete (2011) emphasised that an entity's information technology (IT) system plays an important role in the implementation of new systems such as ABC, which could also be further extended to ABM and ABB. As a result of such an integrated systems approach, the case study will be advanced from the perspective of systems thinking, which is "a holistic perspective that acknowledges that the relationships among system components and between the components and the environment are as important (in terms of system behaviour) as the components themselves" (Monat et al. 2020).

2.2 Systems and Structures of SASSA

SASSA is legislatively mandated to control and oversee the social assistance of South Africa's poor and marginalised people. According to

SASSA (2018), its budget structure encompasses the following key programmes:

- Administration: This entails all the managerial structures and procedures to ensure that SASSA operates effectively;
- Benefits administration and support: This entails the managerial processes and structures focussed on grant operations and policy implementation.

SASSA follows a three-step approach namely customer engagement, capture application and verify applications using IT. This is achieved via the following IT (SASSA 2019):

- The *basic accounting system* operates on a cash basis of accounting and is primarily used for social relief of distress transactions;
- The *enterprise resource planning system* is the primary financial system, and encompass aspects of human capital management, supply chain management, accounting and budgeting and
- The *SOCPEN system* is primarily responsible for the management of social assistance grants.

In providing a contextual background of the scope of SASSA grants, Table 1 below summarises the types of social grants by volume and monetary value over the two most recent two financial years. The number of each grant (i.e. number of clients) and the monetary value thereof are exhibited.

As depicted in Table 1, the number of social grants increased year-on-year except for war veteran, disability and foster care grants. Notably, grant-in-aid represents the highest percentage increase of grant type. Child support grant reflects the greatest number of grant type contrary to that of war veteran. The total value of grants has increased year-on-year in proportion to the number of grants.

Table 2 exhibits SASSA's administration expenditure for the two financial years, 2017/2018 and 2018/2019, respectively.

Notably, there was a reduction in the total expenditure from 2017/2018 to 2018/2019 as is evident from Table 2. Applicable to this study, a volume-based approach to allocate the administration expenditure to the different types of grants, results in an equal amount that is

Table 1 Social grants by type, quantity and monetary value

	Volume (number)		*Monetary value*	
Grant type	**2017/18**	**2018/19**	**2017/18**	**2018/19**
Old age	3,423,337	3,553,317	R64,225,847,005	R70,635,272,034
War veteran	134	92	R3,032,780	R2,391,421
Disability	1,061,866	1,048,255	R20,886,071,889	R22,021,154,883
Grant-in-aid	192,091	221,989	R855,208,997	R840,495,340
Care dependency	147,467	150,001	R2,843,336,250	R3,068,027,810
Foster child	416,016	386,019	R4,950,744,160	R5,114,210,906
Child support	12,269,084	12,452,072	R55,906,388,602	R60,611,568,133
Social relief distress			R484,123,076	R416,719,553
Total	**17,509,995**	**17,811,745**	**R150,154,752,759**	**R162,709,840,080**

Source SASSA (2019)

Table 2 Annual SASSA administration expenditure

Description	*2017/18*	*2018/19*
Personnel costs	R3,027,303,707	R3,173,399,385
Finance cost	R11,916	R35,439
Maintenance and repairs	R25,040,670	R29,565,875
Social Assistance service fee	R2,112,445,337	R1,304,737,089
Administrative expenses	R1,919,767,438	R1,834,641,278
Depreciation	R121,898,923	R118,227,849
Debt impairment	R732,518	R1,444,769
Total	**R7,207,210,509**	**R6,462,051,684**

Source Adapted from SASSA (2019)

assigned to each grant paid. The total expenditure, R7 207 210 509 and R6 462 051 684 divided by the number of grants 17 509 995 and 17 811 745 equal **R411.60**/grant for the 2017/2018 year and **R362.80**/grant for the year 2018/2019. The lowest grant type was for child support, i.e. R380 and R405 per child for the years 2017/2018 and 2018/2019, respectively. The highest grants for these two periods were R1 600 and

R1 695 per person for old age (under 75 years) and R1 620 and R1 715 per person over 75 years (South African National Treasury 2018).

3 Literature Review

Although there is abundant published research on ABC in the private sector, only limited research with a focus on the public sector has been published—even more so within the South African context. In one sub publication, Kee (2012) argues that to effectively deliver public sector services, it is important to properly understand the associated costs in such service delivery. Attempting to expand hereon, this literature review focuses on three aspects of ABC, as follows:

- The first is extent of ABC's implementation. Literature indicated that there are many such implementations in UK and USA-based public sector, i.e. cases in which the resource costs pertaining to public services are accomplished via some kind of a multi-step procedure linked to activity consumption (Stouthuysen et al. 2014). Such findings could be considered as a reflection that many public sector entities consider themselves as adopters of ABM practices. Within the South African context, there seem to be a mindfulness that available resources are becoming scarce, and that cost-efficiency becomes more important. For example, a study by Oseifuah (2014) reported that many South African municipalities accepted that ABC addresses potential inadequacies of conventional systems, and may lead to more effective financial management and efficient service delivery. Nevertheless, it was also found that very few public sector entities (municipalities) actually adopted ABC.
- The second focus is the integration of ABC into the existing systems within a public entity. In this regard, Priyatmo and Akbar (2019) found that ABC can be implemented in the State Treasury Office of Jakarta to calculate unit costs and they concluded that ABC has much to offer an analytical and management tool. They also emphasised however, that ABC is not a magic formula, but only a part of the improvement process of an entity's performance. As mentioned earlier, IT systems play an important role in the implementation of new tools such as ABC and ABM. This IT system provides information for organisational planning of resources, including the

acquiring, implementation and delivering of them. Therefore, the IT system should contain sufficient information about items such as cost objects, resources and activity cost drivers (Cardos and Pete 2011).
- The third focus is on the efficient resource allocation. A study by Bvumbi's (2017) concluded the adoption of ABC has limited impact on the costs of water resource management at the Water Trading Entity (WTE) in South Africa. Therefore, ABC *per se* is not the tool to manage and reduce costs. Managing activities through ABM however, may lead to cost reduction and continuous improvement. Using scarce resources in a cost-effective manner will however, achieve more workable service delivery levels. In this regard, Ngcobo (2019), who investigated ABC as a costing method in South Africa's national electricity supplier, concluded that after implementation, ABC will provide management with a basis to make better management decisions as they will be able to define activities and understand the time required to complete a task.

From the literature it can be concluded that public sector entities are diverse, implying that ABC is probably not equally useful for all. However, in the case of SASSA, it is essential that ABC as an alternative to the conventional costing system should at least be investigated. Especially as management needs more accurate information since, for example, the current volume-based numbers above indicated that it cost SASSA R411.60 (2017/18) and R362.80 (2018/19) on administration to enable them to pay a grant. These numbers are questionable if it is compared, for example to the R380 (2017/18) and R405 (2018/19) grant per child.

Within the context of the purpose of the study, to investigate ABC as an alternative to SASSA's current allocation of indirect costs, the following research questions can be asked:

- What are the dependent factors for the successful implementation of ABC?
- What is the importance of financial information systems in the implementation of ABC?
- What are the employees' perceptions of resource allocation in the ABM environment?

4 Method

Following studies investigating ABC in the public sector, e.g. Bvumbi (2017), Ngcobo (2019), Priyatmo and Akbar (2019), Vazakidis et al. (2010) and Stouthuysen et al. (2014), this case study is classified as a qualitative study utilising semi-structured interviews as the manner by which the data were collected. Initially, ten managers and senior managers within SASSA's financial department and actively involved in costing and budgeting, were purposively sampled. As an interview guide, a semi-structured questionnaire with three research questions were developed, which in turn was deductively converted to a theme, resulting in three main themes. Subsequently, sub-themes were developed inductively for each of the main themes.

MS Excel was used to record the substances of the semi-structured interviews. In order to ensure an accurate reflection of the responses and pre-empt *out-of-context* phrases, content analysis was utilised to analyse the transcripts, during which verbatim information and responses were added for all the participants. The horizontal reflection along the rows of the verbatim responses allowed for comparison pertaining to each of the themes. The themes and sub-themes are as follows:

- Theme 1 analysed the dependent factors for the successful implementation of ABC. This theme consists of three sub-themes, namely:
    - benefits of considering alternative cost allocation systems to traditional costing;
    - key role players to be involved in the ABC implementation initiative and
    - the influence of the accuracy of the available information provided to management to make strategic financial decisions.
- Theme 2 analysed the importance of financial information systems in the implementation of ABC. This theme has two sub-themes, namely:
    - the significance of an ERP system in the implementation of ABC; and
    - the ability to identify the different cost components and its drivers.

- Theme 3 evaluated employees' perceptions of resource allocation in the ABM environment. This theme consists of two sub-themes, namely:
  - the focus on the efficiency and effectiveness in performing activities; and
  - the impact of ABM on the promotion of more effective budgeting practices and strengthening monitoring controls.

The validation of this study was recognised by consulting experts on the subject matter before designing the final sets of interview questions. The credibility of this study was maintained by an extensive explanation of the interpretation method.

5 Results

Data saturation was reached during the fifth interview as no new information was revealed. The researcher was, therefore, confident that the sample of six interviews is sufficient. Such a decision, i.e. the right time to stop collecting more data, is generally dependent on the researcher's sense of what they hear in interviews. As argued by Guest et al. (2006), data saturation could be reached by approximately an estimated six interviews, based on the sample size of the population, while Dibley (2011) argued the richness and thickness of data as being crucial rather than the size.

The summarised results of the analysed data are discussed next, in similar order to the three predetermined themes.

5.1 Theme 1: Dependent Factors for the Successful Implementation of Activity-Based Costing

Sub-theme 1: Benefits of considering an alternative cost allocation system to traditional costing

All participants reflected extensive exposure to the budgeting process applicable to SASSA and it was demonstrated as supported during the interviews: "*The bottom line for government is service delivery, but at the same time we need to ensure that service delivery is being delivered in a cost-effective way and we're getting value for money. And I think when you look at activity-based costing each project or programme then can be unpacked to assist us to understand what is the cost implications*". Participant [2]. In this regard, Angelopoulos and Pollalis (2017), who investigated the Greek Power Public Corporation, argued that the benefit of ABC is that it detects non-value-added activities and consequently limits the wastefulness in this public entity.

Participant [1] affirmed this by stating that "*...and as a public entity we're not necessarily chasing profits, but we still need to render or deliver services in an effective, efficient and economic manner*". This was further elaborated on by participant [5]: "*And also, to deal with the issues of scarce resources as opposed to, or vis a vis, unlimited needs. ABC is one of the tools that can be used to alleviate or to plug the gap between limited resources and unlimited needs*".

Participant [1] supported this view: "*So, with looking at the cost involved in delivering the service that we deliver, we really need to account for each and every cent, not only to account but having ways to cut the cost of delivering a service... so definitely for me ABC is a better method*".

All participants were of the view that it will be more beneficial for SASSA to consider ABC as an alternative costing model to deliver cost-effective and efficient services. This is consistent with the findings by Oseifuah (2014), who argued that the deficiencies associated with traditional approaches when assigning costs to products and services could be overcome by using the ABC method in the public sector.

Sub-theme 2: Key role players that should be involved in ABC implementation initiative

Four (4) participants suggested that, for a successful implementation of ABC, top management must play a key leading role to ensure that lower-level employees are provided with the support required. The majority of participants agreed on a top-to-bottom approach and participant [3] added "*... also the executive authority, which is the minister, you also need her buy-in. Like our mother department basically, let me just say our mother department. We also need them because this is not a SASSA thing only. The mother department is also involved. We also need, and the other key stakeholders, its management accounting and strategy because you cannot go about this thing without strategy and management accounting*".

This supports the findings from literature suggesting that strong top management support is required, as it is nearly impossible to succeed without their full support (Govender 2011; Rundora et al. 2013).

Sub-theme 3: The influence of the accuracy of the available information provided to management to make strategic financial decisions

Accurate and relevant management information is vital in making sound decisions about the organisation, as outlined by the participants. Participant [5] revealed that "*Yes, look, I think the information is accurate in the sense that it is structured, it is based on exactly what kind of information is required both financial and non-financial*". This was supported by participant [3] who said that the information is also available on the intranet, including policies and publications that could be used to make sound decisions. Some participants were, however, not entirely convinced about the accuracy of the information, since participant [1] declared "*And with the current setting yes, some decisions can be made based on that information, but I don't think the information paints the full picture of what is happening within the processes*".

It is evident that, given more accurate or relevant cost information, management can rely on ABC to become more useful as a decision-making tool. Angelopoulos and Pollalis (2017), however, indicated that ABC contributes by preventing distortion of costs of activities by measuring a more exact cost of those activities.

5.2 *Theme 2: The Importance of a Financial Information System in the Implementation of Activity-Based Costing*

Sub-theme 1: The significance of an ERP system (Oracle) in the implementation of ABC

All participants elaborated on using an ERP system as an integral part in the successful implementation of ABC. As suggested by participant [1]: "*So, ERP, Oracle to be exact, would play a big role in collecting, recording and helping analysing the information because it's an ERP system which means that its… The whole organisation components should be integrated in the Oracle system for the purpose then of implementing ABC*".

Participant [2] added: "Activity-based costing will never succeed if we don't have the system to support it. We cannot run activity-based costing on a manual system. Then all you're going to be doing is you're going to be frustrating the management, and you won't get the desired reports that you would need as management information".

The current legacy systems such as BAS and PERSAL would be unable to integrate information, as outlined by participant [5]: "*the ERP is one of the most effective tools of managing resources. And it is flexible, and its real time and it is configured in such a way that it can support the planned financial resources*".

Sub-theme 2: The ability to identify the different cost components and their drivers

Participants agreed that changes in the level of activity are affected by activity cost drivers. These drivers describe the cause-effect correlation between cost objects and activity consumption. Within the context of the public sector, these drivers should be process driven. Wahab et al. (2018) found that these technicality aspects of ABC are critical to influence the success of its implementation. Becker et al. (2009) observed that ABC could assist public organisations to allocate overhead costs accurately to the services. This view was expressed by participant [2]: "*ABC is a financial system but what feeds into that is your policies and your procedures*". Therefore, understanding the activities that drive cost is fundamental to allocate overhead costs more accurately. Kee (2012) argued that the cost of resources used to produce their services must be well understood. This view was emphasised by participant [4]: "*When it comes to ABC system you need to understand the activities, what are the outcomes or output you want to achieve?*"

5.3 Theme 3: Efficient Resource Allocation Is Possible in an Activity-Based Management Environment

Sub-theme 1: The focus on the efficiency and effectiveness in performing activities

Participant [1] stated that "*it's about eliminating those non-value-adding but still get the desired output but now without these other unnecessary or non-value-adding activities because now, those non-value-adding activities now, or the inefficiencies definitely add to the cost as well of the service that we are rendering*".

The ABC system assists in reducing activities that are not adding any value but are consuming resources without providing any benefits. A study by Amir et al. (2012) demonstrated how ABC could help a university to find out where the costs are, what the drivers are and which could be low value-added costs to the cost object.

Participant [2] added: "*Because that's the only way you will find out whether you're being effective or efficient, and not make estimates or assumptions that an official came for five days a week or used a vehicle for two days, but how is it verified? Because then you know whether you've got too many staff, or you've got too many vehicles. You wouldn't know that, and how is it being utilised*". A study by Tuccillo and Agliata (2018) argued that it is crucial to be aware of the problem of scarcity and it is, therefore, necessary to use resources cost-efficiently to achieve goals within the public sector.

Sub-theme 2: The effect of ABM on the promotion of more effective budgeting practices and strengthening monitoring controls

Public organisations are increasingly pressured to provide an account of their actions. This view was emphasised by participant [1] who said, "*Remember your ABC will assist in terms of cutting out inefficiencies, streamlining processes which means then the budget allocation that we're getting is definitely going into the more necessary activities and processes rather than those wastages that are in between*". Participant [2] added: "*So yes, it'll put more responsibility and accountability on cost centres to be more circumspect in terms of what they want and what they deliver. And if there's savings, they need to answer well, why have you got savings? Were you effective or efficient or you just didn't deliver? If you're going to be exceeding the budget what caused that. And activity-based costing will then be able to pinpoint exactly where the issue and the problems are*".

ABC supports transparency and efficiency in managing public sector activities. The study by Baird (2007) revealed that public organisations are reluctant to apply activity management practices to determine the costs of goods and services. Similar to ABC, ABB gives more particular emphasis to overhead activities and their associated costs. It emphasises that, by controlling the level of activity, activity costs could be controlled.

6 Summary and Conclusion

The purpose of this case study was to investigate ABC as an alternative to SASSA's current allocation of administration costs which comprise a significant portion of the total grants. Three research questions were developed, which were converted into themes to guide the interviews. During the interviews, several sub-themes evolved from the three main questions (themes).

Theme 1 analysed the dependent factors for the successful implementation of ABC. From the participants' view, three sub-themes were revealed, namely (i) the benefits of ABC as an alternative to the current system, (ii) the key role players who should be involved in the implementation and (iii) the influence of the accuracy to make strategic financial decisions. In this regard, all participants were of the view that: it will be more beneficial for SASSA to consider ABC as an alternative costing system to deliver services so that it is cost-effective and efficient; SASSA's top management and the Department of Social Development are the key role players; and ABC may become more useful as a decision-making tool as more accurate or relevant cost information are provided as input.

Theme 2 analysed the importance of a financial information system in the implementation of ABC. From the participants' view, two sub-themes should be considered, i.e. the significance of the ERP system and the ability to find different cost components and cost drivers. The participants firstly elaborated on using an ERP system as an integral part in the successful implementation of ABC; and secondly, that changes in the level of activity cost drivers should correlate with a change in the cost objects.

Theme 3 analysed whether efficient resource allocation is possible in an ABM environment. Two sub-themes were revealed: the focus on efficiency and effectiveness, and the promotion of more effective budgeting practices and strengthening monitor controls. The participants emphasised the importance to eliminate non-value-adding activities, and that ABB places particular emphasis on overhead activities and their associated costs, which enables controlling the level of activity.

Considering the above themes, the study concludes that ABC could be implemented as an alternative method in SASSA on a pilot project basis. ABC could be used as a tool to close the gap between scarce resources and unlimited needs. Furthermore, this could be viewed as an attempt to address the challenge of escalating administrative costs by using a contemporary costing system. Moreover, ABC as a stand-alone system may not add sufficient value. It will only be worthwhile if it is implemented within the *context of systems thinking*. Therefore, ABC should be used in conjunction with ABM and ABB. These three systems should further be integrated with the current IT and ERP systems.

Although the results of the study cannot be generalised, the lessons learnt from this study may be beneficial for a prospective public sector ABC-adopter to take cognisance of the factors to be considered for the successful implementation of ABC.

References

Acts see South Africa.

Angelopoulos, M., and Pollalis, Y. 2017. Activity based costing (ABC) as a tool for lean transformation: The case of the Greek Power Public Corporation (PPC). MPRA Paper No. 78848. https://mpra.ub.uni-muenchen.de/78848/1/MPRA_paper_78848.pdf. Date of accessed 15 January 2020.

Amir, A.M., S. Auzair, R. Maelah, and A. Ahmad. 2012. Determination of educational cost in public university—A modified activity-based approach. *World Journal of Social Sciences* 2 (2): 34–48.

Baird, K. 2007. Adoption of activity management practices in public sector organizations. *Accounting and Finance* 47 (4): 551–569.

Becker, J., Bergener, P., and Räckers, M. 2009. Process-based governance in public administrations using activity-based costing. In International Conference on Electronic Government, 176–187, Berlin/Heidelberg, Springer.

Bvumbi, M.N. 2017. Analysis of the implementation of activity-based costing at the water trading entity. Pretoria: UNISA. MPhil, Dissertation.

Cardos, I.R., and S. Pete. 2011. Activity-based costing (ABC) and activity-based management (ABM) implementation—Is this the solution for organizations to gain profitability. *Romanian Journal of Economics* 32 (1): 151–168.

Drury, C. 2018. *Management and cost accounting*, 10th ed. Hampshire: Cengage Learning.

Dibley, L. 2011. Analysing narrative data using McCormack's Lenses. *Nurse Researcher* 18 (3): 13–19.

Govender, D. 2011. The factors that influence the choice between a traditional cost system and an activity-based cost. *International Journal of Arts and Sciences* 4 (15): 241–249.

Guest, G., A. Bunce, and L. Johnson. 2006. How many interviews are enough? An experiment with data saturation and variability. *Field Methods* 18 (1): 59–82.

Hansen, S.C. 2011. A theoretical analysis of the impact of adopting rolling budgets, activity-based budgeting and beyond budgeting. *European Accounting Review* 20 (2): 289–319.

IMF (International Monetary Fund). 2020. Six charts explain South Africa's inequality. https://www.imf.org/en/News/Articles/2020/01/29/na012820six-charts-on-south-africas-persistent-and-multi-faceted-inequality. Date of accessed 16 October 2020.

Johnson, H.T., and R.S. Kaplan. 1987. *Relevance lost: The rise and fall of management accounting*. Boston: Harvard Business School Press.

Kee, R.C. 2012. Measuring & managing the cost of governmental services: A case for time-driven activity-based costing. *The Journal of Government Financial Management* 61 (3): 38–41.

Monat, J., Amissah, M., and Gannon, T. 2020. Practical applications of systems thinking to business. *Systems* 8 (2):14. https://doi.org/10.3390/systems8020014. Date of accessed 16 October 2020.

Ngcobo, N.L. 2019. An evaluation of an activity-driven operational cost accounting framework in an electricity distribution company. MCom, Mini-dissertation, North-West University, Potchefstroom.

Oseifuah, E.K. 2014. Activity-based costing (ABC) in the public sector: Benefits and challenges. *Problems and Perspectives in Management* 12 (4): 581–588.

Priyatmo, T., and R. Akbar. 2019. Analysis of the prospect of implementing activity-based costing (ABC) in governmental organisations: A study at the state treasury office Jakarta IV. *Journal of Accounting and Investment* 20 (1): 1–22.

Rundora, R., T. Ziemerink, and M. Oberholzer. 2013. Activity-based costing in small manufacturing firms: South African study. *Journal of Applied Business Research* 29 (2): 485–498.

SASSA (South African Social Security Agency). 2018. *Annual report 2017/18*. South African Social Security Agency.

SASSA (South African Social Security Agency). 2019. *Annual report 2018/19*. South African Social Security Agency.

South Africa. 1996. Constitution of the Republic of South Africa 1996.

South Africa. 2004. Social Assistance Act No 9 of 2004.

South Africa National Treasury. 2018. *People's guide to the 2018 budget*. http://www.treasury.gov.za/documents/national%20budget/2018/guides/2018%20Peoples%20Guide%20English.pdf. Date of accessed 20 June 2019.

Stouthuysen, K., K. Schierhout, and F. Roodhooft. 2014. Time-driven activity-based costing for public services. *Public Money and Management* 34 (4): 289–296.

Tuccillo, D., and F. Agliata. 2018. The ABC as tool for decision making in public administrations. *Open Journal of Accounting* 7 (2): 125–138.

Vazakidis, A., I. Karagiannis, and A. Tsialta. 2010. Activity-based costing in the public sector. *Journal of Social Sciences* 6 (3): 376–382.

Wahab, A.B.A., M.H.S. Mohamad, and J.M. Said. 2018. The implementation of activity-based costing in the accountant general's department of Malaysia. *Asian Journal of Accounting and Governance* 9: 63–76.

Wachulka-Chan, J. 2019. *Activity-based costing* [Blog post]. 26 August. https://www.practicetestsacademy.com/blog/cima/what-is-behind-the-activity-based-costing. Date of accessed 13 December 2020.

Wang, P., F. Du, D. Lei, and T.W. Lin. 2010. The choice of cost drivers in activity- based costing: Application at a Chinese oil well cementing company. *International Journal of Management* 27 (2): 367–381.

CHAPTER 7

Improving an Automotive Workshop's Profitability Using Lean Management Principles

Pieter Buys and Hardus Oosthuizen

Abstract In a competitive business environment, the automotive industry is finding it challenging to remain competitive and profitable. Lean management has as part of its objectives the improvement of operational processes, better cost management and waste reduction. The aim of this chapter is to analyse the potential impact of activity-based costing and value stream analysis in promoting waste identification and improved profitability in an automotive workshop environment. The research indicated that although the workshop is already performing at an efficiency rate exceeding the original equipment manufacturing benchmark, the redesign of the diagnostic aspect of the workflow could result in further improved efficiencies, with resultant profitability improvements. The results prove the point that any organisation should continuously

P. Buys (✉) · H. Oosthuizen
Management Cybernetics Research Entity, North West University, Potchefstroom, South Africa
e-mail: pieter.buys@nwu.ac.za

P. Buys (ed.), *Designing Cost Management Systems to Support Business Decision-Making*, https://doi.org/10.1007/978-981-16-1751-5_7

strive for optimum operational process redesign and relevant management information generation.

Keywords Activity-based costing · Cost management · Lean management · Value stream analysis · Process-re-engineering

JEL Codes JEL codes · L21 (business objectives) · L23 (organisation of production) · M41 (accounting)

1 Background

The global business environment is a complicated and competitive place to be, and the automotive and related services industry is not immune hereto. The drive for competitiveness and sustainability, even in the automotive industry remains aspects that need to be embraced. This entails the continuous evaluation of operational processes by focusing on waste reduction, cost optimisation, profitability and customer satisfaction (Fei and Isa 2010). It could be argued that an organisation's ability to attain accurate timely information may provide a substantial boost to its own competitive advantage.

Both Fei and Isa (2010) and Walters and Lancaster (2000) make the recommendations that effective managers should focus on optimising its operational business operations and value streams. Furthermore, both Furniss and Spencer (2005) and Poggenpoel (2004) emphasis the fact that inventive business operations may improve organisational value chains and generate relevant cost driver information. It can therefore be argued that when an organisation works more efficiently and reduces waste, it may very well have a positive influence on its financial bottom-line. This establishes the need to evolve conventional measurements to provide more in-depth analyses, performance control and accuracy of cost information. Michael Porter's 1985 published book entitled 'The Competitive Advantage: Creating and sustaining superior performance' introduced the *value chain* concept as highlighting the value-adding aspects throughout the organisation's value stream activities. These value chain activities incorporate (i) *primary* activities such as in- and outbound logistics, operations, marketing and sales, as well as internal services provision, and (ii) *secondary* activities such as procurement, technology support, human capital management and infrastructure. It may be argued that effective management requires that wasteful usage of resources should be minimised.

Lean management is a key management concept with an objective of improving the value stream (operational processes) leading to better cost measurement, operational waste reduction and enhanced sustainability. Within the context of lean management, Tsai (1998) states that activity-based costing (ABC) is a tool available to management that aims to identify deficiencies in conventional costing methods. This may be achieved by analysing operational processes, including related cost drivers and activities (Buyrugan et al. 2009). In analysing operational processes, tools such as value stream mapping (VSM), that visually present the operational processes can play an important role in evaluating the need for certain operational activities and understanding the resource allocation requirements. In doing so, VSM can play a key role in not only the improvement of operational performances, but also in contributing to the longer-term sustainability of the organisation.

2 Research Setting

The Anonymous Motor Group (*AMG*) is a multi-franchised dealership with a fully equipped automotive workshop. The automotive workshop is considered to be key to *AMG*'s business model, providing an important financial contribution through vehicle repairs and maintenance. Within automotive workshops, the time limits for the completion of specific jobs are benchmarked by the original equipment manufacturers (OEM). Illinois Transportation (2007) explains that *time efficiency* entails dividing (i) the workshop hours sold into (ii) the workshop hours worked, meaning that the technician's time efficiency directly relates to his/her profitability. For instance, when a specific service-type job is benchmarked to take 45 minutes, the technician is 100% efficient if he/she takes 45 minutes to complete the job. Completing the job quicker than the benchmark increases the time efficiency rate. To illustrate, if the job is completed in 30 minutes, the technician is 150% efficient {45/30 = 1.5 (or 150%)}.

The effect of better efficiency (in the context of the OEM benchmarks) is that the workshop is able to sell more work hours in a regular workday, and thereby increase its profitability. With time as a key cost driver within the workshop, technologies that enable technicians to obtain *pre-diagnostic* information that can potentially shorten the overall time requirement, should result in operational efficiency improvements, and in turn should result in cost optimisation and profit maximisation. The primary focus of this case study is therefore on finding possible ways to enhance the workshop effectiveness. In doing so, both the current workshop workflow as well as related cost implications will be considered. Since both ABC and VSM focus on analysing and optimising the operational procedures, these complementary tools form the theoretical basis for this case study.

3 Objectives

As stated, the focus of this case study is on the optimisation of the current operational and cost management processes pertaining to AMG's workshop. Considering the above background information, the primary research objective is formulated as follows:

- Can lean management tools and concepts provide management with a feasible way to identify inefficient operational practices as a way to improve the workshop efficiency and profitability of technicians in workshop?

In attempting to attain the above objective, several secondary objectives are identified, as presented below:

- Identifying and considering key management tools that may enable process improvements, such as lean management principles, the costing approach and process analysis;
- Unpacking the current state of AMG workshop's processing and costing approach and
- Using the above identified tools to propose enhancements to the workshop business model.

The case study is presented in the following manner. Firstly, the essence of lean management, ABC and VSM principles are highlighted within the context of workshop profitability. Secondly, the case study information and analysis is provided by firstly analysing the current scenario including the current basic cost structure and efficiency, which will then be followed by the re-thinking of the value stream and the evaluation of the potential impact of VSM re-alignment. Finally, some conclusions and recommendations will be provided.

4 Building Blocks of Process Improvement

4.1 Introduction

Since organisations aiming to achieve sustainable business success, must provide quality products and services at competitive prices (Huang et al. 2013), effective cost management becomes crucial in not only profitability, but also in ensuring quality service delivery. Smith et al. (2012) argues from a different perspective and states that incorrect product data may result in increased costs. Even though many historically bad decisions may be blamed for organisational non-sustainability, the underlying theoretical point of departure of this case study is that, in terms of costs, sustainability does not require *cost-cutting* per se, but rather effective *cost management*. The subsequent sections start with a consideration of the integrated nature of several key underlying management concepts, namely:

- Lean management principles, which aims to enhance customer centricity through continual improvement through the reduction of waste and closely monitoring upstream and downstream practises (Liker and Morgan 2006);
- ABC that build thereon and is a management approach that analyses operational activities and assigns indirect costs thereto (Brewer et al. 2010) and
- VSM, which in turn is a visual tool depicting operational processes, thereby providing an opportunity to analyse such processes and identify areas of improvement (Jacobs and Chase 2013).

4.2 Lean Management

According to Apel et al. (2007), Henri Ford popularised the concept of *flow production* in the early 1900s by using reliably transposable components with standardised work processes. Post-World War I, the Toyota Production System (TPS) presented the concept of lean manufacturing, which provided the fundamentals thereof not only to manufacturing organisations, but also to other industries such as the financial and medical industries (Liker and Morgan 2006). The concept of lean management is fundamentally supported by three management aspects, namely operations, administration and strategy (Apel et al. 2007), which all need to work in synergy in order to be successful (Liker and Morgan 2006; Womack and Jones 1996). Furthermore, according to Liker and Morgan (2006), such an integrated management approach consists of principles such as:

- Just-in-time (JIT), which promotes efficient resource flow and the ability to provide the resources on the exact time when it is needed.
- Jidoka, which refers to the intelligence required to ensure quality and is achieved by identifying any deviation from the norm and stopping production immediately in order to rectify possible problems.
- Stable and standardised processes, which aim to flatten workflows and to identify possible improvement opportunities.

In its essence therefore, lean management has as its foundational philosophy the elimination of wasted resources. In the context of this case study therefore, the aim is to identify and possibly eliminate wastage of resources, whether in the form of materials, time consumption or redundant activities.

4.3 Activity-Based Costing

Due to automation, engineering-driven proficiencies and customer-focused strategies, the portion of overhead costs to total (operational) cost increased during the twentieth century, which, according to Kaplan and Anderson (2013) came with financial implications of accumulated overhead costs by adding more focused dimensions to business operations. Alfonso and Santana (2016) is of the opinion that modern costing systems should be able to accommodate all the diversity and complexities of contemporary production and business procedures. In this context, the concept of ABC is essentially a *rate and performance measurement process* of cost objects and operational processes, and as such, it is a costing methodology whereby activities are measured by means of resource absorption (CIMA 2005; Nachtmann and Al-Rifai 2010). ABC aims to support strategic management (Alfonso and Santana 2016), and is not only considered as a more accurate costing technique, but it is also correspondingly a co-ordination of measuring standards and actual costs (Kaplan and Anderson 2013), which could offer better traceability of costs to operational processes.

Notwithstanding its promise, the proper implementation of an ABC system is often very costly and difficult to establish (Brewer et al. 2010; Buyrugan et al. 2009), leaving management to decide whether the associated implementation and operational costs are too high when considering the expected benefits. Time-driven activity-based costing (TDABC) in turn, may provide an alternate ABC approach by avoiding the need for intensive data-collection efforts to map resources (costs) to operational processes. TDABC is an approach with the aim of reducing the implementation barriers of conventional ABC (Kaplan and Anderson 2013; Szychta 2010). It allocates resource overheads to cost objects using a dual approach, which (i) calculates the so-called *cost rate* by dividing the cost of capacity supplied with the practical capacity of the resources supplied, and then (ii) using this cost rate as the driver to estimate the demand that each cost object, customer or product needs. Considering the aforementioned, TDABC essentially calculates the cost objects' cost with ***time*** as the cost driver. Time therefore becomes the resource cost allocator directly linked to different objects during the process flow (Alfonso and Santana 2016). This costing method accommodates unique customer orders because it allocates time spent on individual processes and individually allocates costs of the time spent on the process. One of the objectives of this case study entails the proper identification and determination of supportive and relevant cost information in support of enhanced decision support.

4.4 Value Stream Mapping

The increasing cost of controlling operations and labour is forcing many organisations to focus on areas where they can effectively manage costs and reduce waste. However, identifying lead times, defects and other waste can be a taxing and often time-consuming exercise. To assist herein, VSM both analyses and visually depicts the operational processes in the so-called *value* stream. The concept of value is directly linked to a ***monetary*** value and the willingness of customers to exchange their money for the product or service offered (Liker and Morgan 2006). It is therefore important to note that not all processes add value to the final product or service, and according to Apel et al. (2007), non-value-adding processes

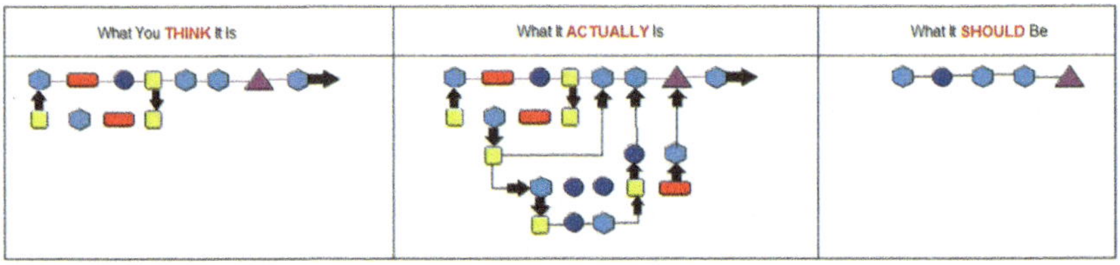

Fig. 1 Three operational process dimensions

need to be identified and eliminated. During the VSM process, it is important to map the process objectively as a true transparency of the reality and not as subjectively perceived or subconsciously wanted (as indicated in Fig. 1):

It is therefore imperative that, throughout this process of operational analysis and mapping, the operational process followed is continually evaluated within the context of whether the right things are still being done right. In support of the lean management objectives, the current workflow in *AMG*'s workshop would therefore be scrutinised to identify possible areas of improvement and reduction of resource wastage.

5 Research Method

The research was conducted in a case study format, which, according to Yin (2014) is an empirical research method focussed on a specific topic set in its real life environment. This particular case study is supplemented by way of the preceding literature overview of supporting management techniques. In terms of the empirical case analysis, it is conducted based on lean management concepts such as ABC principles and VSM procedures. According to Yin (2014), case studies are typically divided into (i) descriptive cases that aim to describe behaviours from practice, (ii) exploratory cases that has the objective of exploring specific procedures and (iii) causal cases with the objective to identify some *cause and effect* relationship between the applicable variables. This case study is considered as an exploratory case, and analyses the current operational processes within *AMG*'s workshop with specific reference to the diagnostic aspect of vehicle servicing.

Thirty-five diagnostic job cards of cases meeting the technical OBD (see later) and OEM related work requirements, have been identified and analysed in order to establish the current, standardised times of the technicians. The pre-diagnostic phase was then be re-modelled and the time efficiency re-calculated to gauge the potential effect of the VSM intervention on the technicians' efficiency rate, and thus potentially the workshop's profitability. Essentially therefore, the case study reports on a current situational analysis, in comparison to a potentially enhanced situational analysis (given the same data set). As such then, the study aims to calculate technician costs, revenue and profitability with *time* as the cost driver, and then also to evaluate operational processes and possibly re-engineer the current diagnostic process within the workshop environment.

In terms of validation, *AMG*'s financial management team validated the model by incorporating the improvement suggestions.

6 The Case of *AMG*

6.1 Problem Definition: Current Scenario

The preceding sections provided some theoretical support for the case study, the objective of which is to investigate, in light of the lean management concepts, the potential impact thereof on the profitability within *AMG*'s workshop. As mentioned earlier, the data presented in this section is based on an analysis of 35 job cards presenting separate but similar jobs within the workshop. The problem definition roadmap will consider the current scenario, including the current workflow and technician-related efficiency, costs, revenues and profitability, before attempting to identify areas of wastage.

Current Workflow

The focus of the value stream analysis is on the current diagnostic process followed, and will only consist of the time data of the actual diagnostic process. Refer to Fig. 2 below for a basic outlay of the value stream of *AMG*'s workshop. Curently, the process starts with the pre-picking of parts, the physical booking of the vehicle, the technician retrieving the vehicle from the parking bay and then conducting the diagnostics. If additional parts are required, such parts are picked (if applicable) and the repairs are conducted, after which the vehicle is cleaned and returned to the customer. An analysis of the workflow and job card data indicated that there is a lead time of two hours during the diagnostics process, due

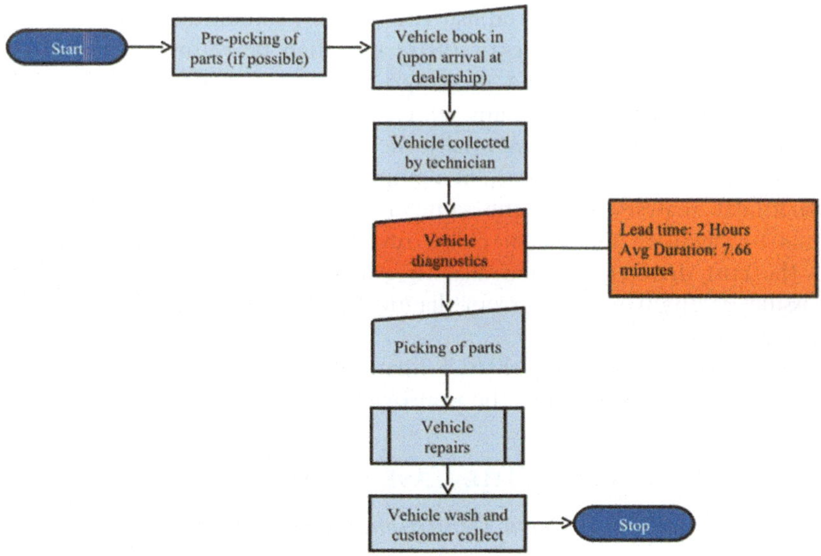

Fig. 2 VSM with diagnostics as focal point

to the fact that the vehicles remain in the parking bays without receiving any attention.

Note that the OEM benchmarked time starts as soon as the vehicle is booked in, before the applicable technician even collects the vehicle. This lead time is mainly due to current work in progress that needs to be completed before an open working bay is available to lift the next vehicle.

Technician Efficiency

As stated, the benchmark for each job type within the franchise workshop is predetermined by the applicable OEM. Based on these predetermined OEM times, the benchmarked time for completion of the actual jobs is determined, which in turn, provides a standardised measurement to which the technicians must exhibit their skills. Depending on the technicians' skills level however, their efficiency rates can fluctuate. Therefore, as the point of departure for the case analysis, the efficiency rate of *AMG*'s technicians is determined as follows:

$$ER = Bt_{OEM} / t \quad (1)$$

where: ER –Efficiency rate
Bt_{OEM}–OEM Benchmark time requirement
t–Actual time consumed

Although each individual job under consideration has a specific time allocated to it, for illustrative purposes the average hours are used, resulting in an average (normalised) *ER*. Therefore, if the technician takes longer than the OEM benchmark, the *ER* will reflect a ratio of < 1, which in effect means that *AMG* is losing money due to the loss of any *efficiency-driven* revenue opportunities. Inversely, when the *ER* is > 1, the technician is more efficient. In this case study, the *ER* calculation information is presented in the table below, highlighting the current technician efficiency.

It is seen above that the OEM benchmark time to complete the sampled jobs came to 83.08 hours, while in actuality the technicians completed the jobs in 73.62 hours (based on the data per the job cards), thereby establishing the *ER* at 1.13. It can therefore be deduced that in the current environment, the workshop already operates at an average *ER* of 13% over the benchmark.

Technician Costs
The workshop manager indicated that the mean salary of a technician amounted to ZAR[1] 12,500 per month (excluding overtime). For illustrative and consistency purposes, it is taken that there is an average of 20 working days per month, and that a normal working day consists of eight (8) hours per day, including a lunch break of one (1) hour. For purposes of this case study, therefore, the cost per technician is based on seven (7) actual working hours per day, which amounts to ZAR 89.29 per hour as illustrated in the table below.

Therefore, since the technicians are already more efficient than the OEM benchmark (refer Table 1), the workshop already has more potentially *sellable* (or billable) hours available in a working day. As illustrated in Table 2 above, at an *ER* of 1.13, the effective hourly technician cost decreases to ZAR 79.01 (or $1/1.13 \times$ ZAR 89.29) per hour.

[1] ZAR refers to South African Rand, which is the local currency.

Table 1 Average technician efficiency

BtOEM	83.08 hours
t	73.62 hours
ER	1.13

Table 2 Effective technician cost

Monthly salary cost	ZAR 12,500.00
Rate per working hour	ZAR 89.29
(Potential) *ER*	1.13
(Potential) labour rate/hour	ZAR 79.01

Table 3 Effective technician revenue

(OEM) benchmark labour rate/hour	ZAR 550.00
ER	1.13
(Effective) labour rate/hour	ZAR 621.50

Technician Revenue

Being a franchised dealership, the billable hourly rates are prescribed by the franchisor. Revenue income in a workshop environment is generated by the number of hours *sold*, and is paid for by either the warranty or after-sale plans' underwriters (if applicable), or otherwise payable by the customer. At the time of the study, there were six (6) technicians employed at *AMG*, with an average labour rate of ZAR 550 per hour. Table 3 below indicates the effective impact of the *ER* on the labour rate.

It is seen that although the billable rate amounts to ZAR 550 per hour, the *ER* of 1.13 results in an effective rate of ZAR 621.50 per technician hour. Therefore, due to the actual efficiency being 13% above the benchmark, the technician should be able to do 13% more work within an hour, and consequently potentially generate additional revenue over and above the benchmark norm.

Technician Profitability

Since the technicians' salaries are fixed, the window of opportunity to increase profitability rests on the efficiency of the workshop technicians. In gauging the profitability, therefore, Table 4 below indicates that, at 100% efficiency in accordance with the OEM benchmark, AMG's profit

Table 4 Profitability analysis at OEM benchmark levels

Labour revenue/hour	ZAR 550.00
Labour cost/hour	ZAR 89.29
Labour profit/hour	ZAR 460.71
Profitability %	83.8%

Table 5 Profitability analysis at effective *ER* levels

Labour revenue/hour	ZAR 621.50
Labour cost/hour	ZAR 79.01
Labour profit/hour	ZAR 542.49
Profitability %	87.3%

margin in terms of labour should be 83.8% and its hourly profitability is ZAR 460.71 per hour.

Taking current efficiency into account, Table 5 below indicates that at the current 13% efficiency over the OEM benchmark, *AMG*'s actual profit margin is effectively 87.3%, with its hourly profitability increasing to ZAR 542.49 per hour.

Based on the above data in Table 5, with the current *ER* of 1.13, the workshop is currently able to increase its profitability by around three and a half (3.5) percentage points (from an 83.8% profit rate to an 87.3% profit rate).

Reducing Wasted Time

As explained by Palumbo and Dyer (2008), contemporary mobile technologies may help with streamlining operational processes and provide a significant return on investment (ROI) by achieving higher efficiency in completing tasks by decreasing operational costs, reducing data errors and loss and also by improving consumer retention through better customer service. According to Tahat et al. (2012), the implementation of on-board diagnostic systems (OBD) dates back to the 1960s. The application of this technology has since expanded, for example since 1996 all vehicles sold in the US had OBD capabilities. The current standard (OBDII) stipulates the type of connector and its communication with the protocols from the vehicle's OBD, and functions among one of five protocols: (i) SAE-J1850 pulse width modulation; (ii) SAE-J1850 variable pulse width modulation; (iii) ISO-14230 keyword protocol 2000; (iv) ISO-15765 Controller Area Network (CAN) or (v) ISO-9141–2 protocol. (Note:

All vehicles used in this study used the ISO-9141–2 protocol). The 16-pin (2 × 8) J1962 female OBDII connector is typically located within close proximity of the vehicle's steering column. The key objective of this technology is to enable an automotive workshop to receive real-time diagnostic information of the vehicles, reset fault codes, while accurately guiding technicians to rectify and/or replace the faulty parts. In the *AMG* case study, although these diagnostic tools are available, the current diagnostic process is not optimised to its full benefit, which may result in less than optimum service delivery.

In terms of re-thinking the workflow, the basic workflow information (illustrated in Fig. 3 below) remains essentially the same as before with the exception that the diagnostic process is moved one step earlier. This should eliminate the two-hour lead time, because the OBD diagnostics of a vehicle can be conducted while the repairs on the other vehicles continue. The diagnostic process is calculated within the available benchmarked time; however, the actual diagnostics are done by making use of the OBD port and a diagnostic device detecting fault codes from the vehicle's on-board computer. Furthermore, this task does not need to be

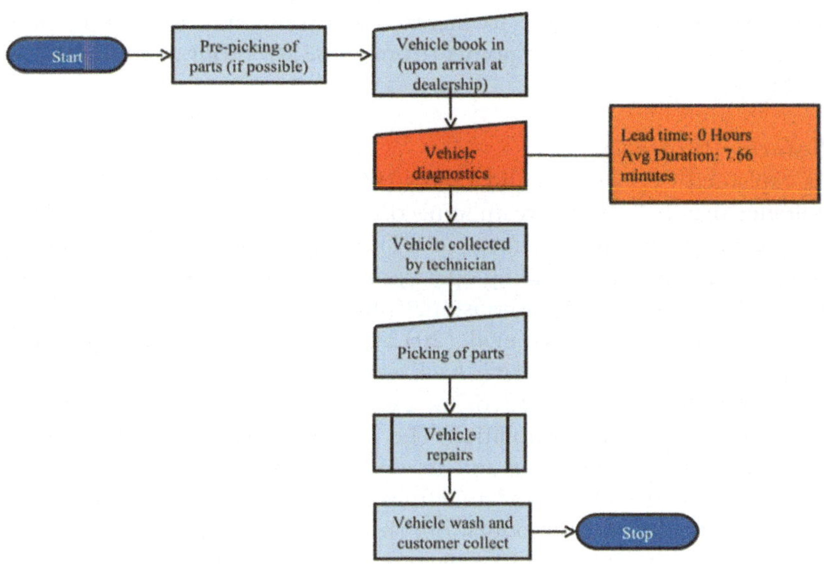

Fig. 3 Revised VSM with diagnostics as focal point

Table 6 Revised time efficiency calculation

Bt_{OEM}	83.08 hours
(Potential) t	65.86 hours
(Potential) ER	1.26

done by the technicians (as currently happens), but can be completed by the service advisors or alternatively a specialised diagnostic employee, as soon as the vehicle has been booked in.

Shifting the time allocation from the technician by removing this function from their responsibility, while only providing them with the comprehensively conducted pre-diagnostics information, increases the technicians' time availability, it was found that it allowed the technicians to complete jobs in 7.66 minutes (on average) faster.

6.2 *Problem Reduction: Revisiting the Value Stream*

Following a similar roadmap as per the above section, a re-designed value stream consideration will be based on a consideration of the costs relative to the revenue and then especially in the context of technician specific data such as technician costs, revenue and profitability.

Cost/revenue Calculation

After revising the value stream, the *potential* time-efficiency calculation per technician can be determined. The potential *ER* can be improved more than the current actual *ER*, with the analysis indicating that with some minor process improvement suggestions, the jobs in the sample could have been completed in 65.86 hours, as opposed to 73.62 hours under the current scenario.

Referring to Table 6 above, the post-VSM intervention indicated that the *ER* of the technicians could improve to 1.26 (or 26% over the benchmark), in comparison to 1.13 under the current scenario. Since the billable labour rates per hour and expenses remained fixed, the technician could therefore further increase the revenue potential per hour resulting in increased profitability by becoming even more efficient.

Potential Technician Costs

Table 7 below re-calculates the cost per technician with the potential *ER* noted. The table confirms that the monthly salary per technician

Table 7 Potential technician cost

Monthly salary cost	ZAR 12,500.00
Rate per working hour	ZAR 89.29
(Potential) *ER*	1.26
(Potential) labour rate/hour	ZAR 70.86

Table 8 Revised revenue potential

(OEM) benchmark labour rate/hour	ZAR 550.00
(Potential) *ER*	1.26
(Potential) labour rate/hour	ZAR 693.00

and working days remained constant (i.e. labour rate of ZAR 89.29 per hour). However, with the potential *ER* at 1.26, the cost per technician is re-calculated at ZAR 70.86 per hour.

Potential Technician Revenue

Table 8 below re-calculates the potential revenue after the intervention. Even though the labour rates (benchmarked) remained constant, bringing the post *ER* into the equation may result in a revenue increase to ZAR 693.00 per hour, which compares favourably with the R621.5 under the current scenario.

Potential Technician Profitability

Table 9 constitutes the revised profitability analysis of the post-value stream intervention. The average efficiency rate is predetermined to increase further from the current 1.13–1.26, resulting in the predetermined labour cost per technician decreasing from the current ZAR 79.01 to a possible ZAR 70.86.

Table 9 Revised profitability potential

Labour revenue/hour	ZAR 693.00
Labour cost/hour	ZAR 70.86
Labour profit/hour	ZAR 622.14
Profitability %	89.8%

After the VSM process was revisited with the diagnostics function changing to one step earlier, it resulted in a positive change in technician profitability over the current efficiency (i.e. from 83.8% to a potential 89.8%, or then an improvement of 7.16%).

7 Concluding Discussion

7.1 *Research Synopsis*

The case study analysed the workflow of *AMG*'s workshop operations with specific reference to its diagnostic procedures. The primary research objective was to consider whether lean management tools can enhance technician profitability and possibly identify waste incurrences in current operational processes. Building hereon, a further consideration was whether pre-diagnostics would increase the average efficiency rate of the technicians. For this case study, the current diagnostic process was evaluated with the diagnostic procedure as focal point, attempting to identify waste. The fixed technician cost to company (salary) was used as the basis for the cost calculations and the billable time as the driver for the revenue calculation.

In achieving the research objectives, the current cost and revenue values were determined by making use of the data received from the workshop manager(s). It was found that both ABC and VSM concepts would enable *AMG* to not only better grasp the reality of their current workshop workflow, but also identify areas of waste and an opportunity to enhance profitability. Using the same data set of 35 job cards, the situational analysis can be summarised as follows (Table 10):

Table 10 Summative situational analysis

	Current scenario	*Enhanced scenario*
Technician efficiency	13%	26%
Technician cost per hour	R 79.01/hour	R 79.86/hour
Technician revenue per hour	R 621.50/hour	R 693.00/hour
Technician profitability	87.3%	89.8%

It was noted that the major influence on the *ER* was the lead time incurred before the diagnostics process, in which the technician personally conducted the diagnostics after the vehicle has been clocked-in. It was also found that there is ample time to conduct the diagnostic before the technician's time commences on the vehicle using readily available OBD technologies, which improved the potential *ER* achievable. With the current objective of reducing waste, the project restructured the current diagnostic process and recalculated the *ER* rate, which indicated a significant increase, which directly affected the profitability potential of the workshop.

With the integration of lean management concepts, the analysis aspect can be enhanced within *AMG*. Due to the case study's close link to 'working hours', opting to integrate TDABC as a management tool may provide management with better predetermined cost and revenue information. In addition, due to the barrier of implementing conventional ABC, it is suggested that considering TDABC is also a potentially easier and less complicated approach to ABC, which should be integrated into the current ERP system.

The study also integrated VSM as a continuous evaluation framework that can enable the workshop to improve processes by optimising workflow. Lead time was identified as a (preventable) waste aspect during the diagnostic process that was followed. The elimination thereof as such should lead to increased profits or a more attractive value proposition for consumers. VSM should become an ingrained practice incorporated within *AMG* environment, and should provide management with valuable insights on improving the current processes.

7.2 Conclusion

Considering the findings, it is evident that, if management is provided with tools, they may be able to improve and measure performance better and by challenging the status quo of operations they can lever significant results by making small amendments. Pre-diagnostics will indeed increase the average efficiency rate of technicians within the workshop.

Although it can be seen that management tools and philosophies may provide great opportunities to enhance profitability, a truly sustainable organisation should be striving for more than just being profitable. As such, *AMG* must be cognisant of the fact that it does not operate in a vacuum, and that it is part of a greater societal system, which should not be overlooked in its profitability efforts. Therefore, a key aspect in the re-design of the operations is to take cognisance of how it impacts on the work environment. If adverse pressure is placed on the technicians to work faster and generate more profit, the *enhancement* drive may backfire in the form of dissatisfied technicians, followed by a drop in work quality and then ultimately in declining customer satisfaction.

7.3 Limitations

It should be noted that this case study is pertinent to this specific entity, and that generalisations of the finding should be avoided. It should also be noted that the challenges that these management tools pose are firstly that accurate data has to be provided in order to calculate reliable data. Furthermore, during the process evaluation, it is important to be unbiased, which really challenges the processes. If accurate data is received and objectivity to improve business is present, a merged TDABC and VSM structure can add immense value to business operations.

References

Alfonso, P., and A. Santana. 2016. Application of the TDABC model in the logistics process different capacity cost rates. *Journal of Industrial Engineering and Management* 9 (5): 1003–1019.

Apel, W., J.Y. Li, and V. Walton. 2007. Value stream mapping for lean manufacturing implementation. Wuhan, China: Huazhong University of Science & Technology (Thesis—PhD).

Brewer, P.C., R.H. Garrison, and E.W. Noreen. 2010. *Introduction to managerial accounting*. New York: McGraw-Hill.

Buyrugan, N., H. Nachtmann, and S. Celikkol. 2009. A model for integrated implementation of activity-based costing and radio frequency identification technology in manufacturing. *International Journal of RF Technologies* 1 (2): 114–130.

CIMA (Chartered Institute of Management Accounting). 2005. Official terminology. 2nd ed. Oxford: CIMA Publishing.

Fei, Z.Y., and C.R. Isa. 2010. Behavioural and organizational variables affecting the success of ABC success in China. *African Journal of Business Management* 4 (111): 2302–2308.

Furniss, T., and M. Spencer. 2005. Activity-based costing: From a provider's perspective. *Official Journal of the Institute of Municipal Finance Officers* 5 (3): 27–28.

Huang, S.Y., H.J. Chen, A.A. Chiu, and C.P. Chen. 2013. The application of the theory of constraints and activity-based costing to business excellence: The case of automotive electronics manufacture firms. *Total Quality Management & Business Excellence* 25 (5–6): 532–545.

Illinois Transportation. 2007. Calculating efficiency, utilization and productivity for auto repair job. Illinois Transportation, Distribution and Logistics Math and Science Project.

Jacobs, R.F., and R.B. Chase. 2013. *Operations and supply chain management*, 13th ed. New York: McGraw-Hill/Irwin.

Kaplan, R.S., and S.R. Anderson. 2013. *Time-driven activity-based costing*. Boston, MA.: Harvard Business Press.

Liker, J.K., and J.M. Morgan. 2006. The Toyota way in services: The case of lean product development. *Academy of Management Perspectives* 20 (2): 5–20.

Nachtmann, H., and M.H. Al-Rifai. 2010. An application of activity based costing in the air conditioner manufacturing industry. *The Engineering Economist* 49: 221–236.

Palumbo, S. and N. Dyer. 2008. Maximizing mobile worker productivity. Boston, MA: Yankee Group Research.

Poggenpoel, J.P. 2004. Die implementering van n aktiwiteitsgebaseerde kostestelsel in n finansiële diensmaatskappy (The implementation of an activity-based costing system in financial services company). Johannesburg: RAU (Dissertation—MCom).

Smith, B.K., H. Nachtmann, and E.A. Pohl. 2012. Improving healthcare supply chain processes via data standardization. *Engineering Management Journal* 24 (1): 3–10.

Szychta, A. 2010. Time-driven activity-based costing in service industries. *Social Sciences* 1 (67): 49–60.

Tahat, A., A. Said, F. Jaouni, and W. Qadamani. 2012. Android-based universal vehicle diagnostic and tracking system. (Consumer Electronics (ISCE), 2012 IEEE 16th International Symposium on IEEE, 2012).

Tsai, W. 1998. Quality cost measurement under activity-based costing. *International Journal of Quality & Reliability Management* 15 (7): 719–752.

Walters, D., and G. Lancaster. 2000. Implementing value strategy through the value chain. *Management Decision* 38 (3): 160–178.

Womack, J.P., and D.T. Jones. 1996. *Lean thinking: Banish waste and create wealth in your corporation*. New York: Simon & Schuster.

Yin, R. 2014. Case study research design and methods. Sage Publishing.

CHAPTER 8

Concluding Comments

Pieter Buys

Abstract It is important to have effective cost management systems in place that are able to generate relevant cost management information. Key hereto is said systems' ability to embrace the concepts of feedback and control in support of organisational objectives. Six case studies illustrated these concepts; firstly, in developing of a cost management system for water recycling facility fabricator, and secondly by designing a budgetary system for a mining engineering concern. These were followed up by designing cost management systems for a digital technology services provider, a medical insurance services provider and a public sector services provider. Finally the case of a re-designed value stream for an automotive services provider was also shared.

Keywords Budgetary system · Cost management system · Organisational strategy

P. Buys (✉)
Management Cybernetics Research Entity, North West University, Potchefstroom, South Africa
e-mail: pieter.buys@nwu.ac.za

P. Buys (ed.), *Designing Cost Management Systems to Support Business Decision-Making*, https://doi.org/10.1007/978-981-16-1751-5_8

1 Background

Effective cost management is arguably one of the key foundations of effective business management. As alluded to in these case studies, the *management of costs* could be somewhat misleading concept. It can be argued the incurrence of costs is the result of certain activities and operations, which in turn are the results of certain management decisions. Effective cost management therefore comes down to (at least in some part) the effective management of activities and operations. Designing a cost management systems from a systems theory perspective therefore makes logical business sense.

Conceptually speaking, the attainment of specific organisational goals requires certain outputs, which in turn requires certain inputs. Key to such goal-driven objectives is the concept of systems and of the cybernetics feedback loop, the latter which is a key enabler of corrective actions. This loop entails the:

- Continuous monitoring of the environment;
- Processing of the environmental information and then
- Reacting thereto, either by adapting or accepting the current course of action.

By incorporating the feedback loop concept into a (organisational) system, one can argue that even the most basic system could have multiple cybernetic feedback loops. The cybernetic concepts of feedback, control and being goal-driven implies the active incorporation of stakeholder feedback, even to extend potentially changing organisational strategies and operations. These principles are by implication integrally part of the proper understanding of effective cost management and its place in managing the organisational system.

2 Summative Findings

In support of the above, the ***first case study*** considered the case of a water recycling fabrication facility and found that although the organisation operates in an engineering domain as three distinct systems, there is a common business objective. Nevertheless, in reality there was very limited analysis and management effort directed towards effective cost management, which essentially resulted in the guessing of the potential indirect cost implications. The research suggests that the current costing application worksheets be adjusted in order to enable the incorporation of the operational information in the costing framework, and that absorption costing be used as the costing approach, with job costing as the basis for the costing system.

Also in the engineering domain, the ***second case study*** had a more technologically sophisticated focus. The challenge in this instance was found in the geographically diverse reach of the organisation's footprint, and the challenge it faces in effectively communicating and sharing pertinent information between sites across the world. The study considered various Industry 4.0 technologies, and found that specific technologies such as big data, simulation and cyber-physical systems, can very effectively be used to design a budgeting control framework to strengthen internal governance by improving cost management through better communication and real-time decision-making.

Moving further into the 4th Industrial Revolution sphere, the ***third case study*** focussed on a digital technology services organisation. As is typical in many fast growing organisations, the initial strategies were focussed on growth, and not on effective cost management *per se*. Nevertheless, the organisation reached a stage where its size warrants re-thinking its cost management policies and practices. The research concluded that time-driven activity-based costing could be implemented as an alternative costing method by linking it with their ERP system. What was also important to note is that a focus on costs may result in a reduction of costs, effectively enabling the organisation to save money and reinvest such savings back into its growth strategies.

The financial implications of health care is a topical issue globally. With the advent of the reconstruction of the South African health care industry, the ***fourth case study*** centred on a cost management framework within a South African medical scheme service provider. The case study illustrated that by following a systematic systems thinking approach, contributes substantially in ensuring the design of an effective cost management framework. The case study highlighted the key iterations, from the *proof of concept*, through the design and development of both *Alpha* and *Beta* versions, of how this bespoke cost management framework was developed, tested and implemented.

A further burning issue in many developing countries is the social security aspect. The ***fifth case study*** considered the effective cost management of the South African Social Security Agency (SASSA). Governmental institutions are typically not known for their cost efficiencies, and SASSA is perhaps a case in point with substantial amounts of money expended in the administration of its services. The study concluded that ABC principles could be an alternative costing method in SASSA—even if only as an initial pilot project. Based on the research, it is important for a prospective ABC adopter to take cognisance of the factors to be considered for the successful implementation of ABC.

The ***final case study*** considered the application of lean management principles on the potential profits and costs within an automotive workshop. To this effect the applicable value stream was analysed and evaluated. The evidence indicated that although the workshop is already exceeding pertinent OEM efficiency benchmarks, re-considering the diagnostic aspect of the workflow could result in doubling the current operational efficiencies, with a resultant improvement in profitability.

3 Closing

Per the primary objective as set out in the first chapter, the focus of this book was on whether an integrative systems approach to cost management could result in better and more effective decision-making. As was illustrated in each of the case studies, many managers and organisations realised that costs, and the understanding thereof, are important in the context of their specific organisations, and that costs must not be seen in isolation, but rather as a key component in the organisational system. An integrated systems approach to cost management should therefore be the departure point when designing cost management systems.

Index

A
Action design research (ADR), 7, 19, 35, 44, 45, 59, 60, 68, 75, 82, 92, 93, 101
Activity-based budgeting (ABB), 109, 110, 120, 121
Activity-based costing (ABC), 8, 9, 17, 64, 67, 109, 110, 113–115, 117–121, 127–132, 141, 142, 148
Activity-based management (ABM), 109, 110, 113, 114, 116, 120, 121

B
Budgeting, 7, 8, 43, 45–50, 52–55, 57–60, 72, 110, 111, 115, 116, 120, 121, 147

C
Corporate governance, 42, 43
Cost management, 5–9, 12–20, 26, 32, 35–37, 66, 67, 92, 93, 101, 103, 110, 128, 129, 146–148

E
Engineering management, 13, 23

H
Healthcare service providers, 89–93

I
Industry 4.0 technologies, 7, 43, 45–49, 52–55, 58, 59, 147
Internal control, 42, 43, 49, 59

P. Buys (ed.), *Designing Cost Management Systems to Support Business Decision-Making*, https://doi.org/10.1007/978-981-16-1751-5

L
Lean management, 9, 127–130, 132, 133, 141, 142, 148

M
Medical costs, 89
Multinational company(ies), 7, 42, 59

N
Network channelling, 8, 89–91, 94, 97, 104

P
Process-re-engineering, 133
Public sector costing, 109

S
Service provider networks, 8
Social grants, 8, 109, 111, 112
Systems theory, 3, 7, 64, 66, 81, 82, 146

T
Time-driven activity-based costing (TDABC), 67, 72–74, 82, 83, 131, 142, 143, 147
Traditional costing, 12, 115, 116

V
Value stream analysis, 133

The manufacturer's authorised representative in the EU is Springer
Nature Customer Service Centre GmbH, Europaplatz 3, 69115 Heidelberg,
Germany. If you have any concerns regarding our products, please
contact ProductSafety@springernature.com

Printed and bound by CPI Group (UK) Ltd, Croydon, CR0 4YY

30/09/2026

02225262-0001